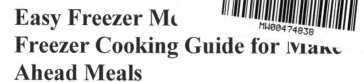

Easy Freezer Me
Freezer Cooking Guide for Make
Ahead Meals

Family Cooking Series
by Debbie Madson
www.kids-cooking-activities.com
© Copyright 2014

Contents

Enjoy the convenience of freezer meals

When you've had a busy day, frantically handling a thousand activities relating to your job and your kids, wouldn't it be great to come home to a ready-made meal that's both nutritious and delicious? We can show you how you can stock up on a wide range of family-friendly meals and snacks that are ready for defrosting and serving any time. Freezer meals are ready when you are – when you're too tired after a long day to think about dinner; when you're home late and just want something quickly; or when the fresh meal you planned just doesn't tempt you. Freezer meals do take some planning but you will see they are worth the little extra effort when they come through for you in an emergency!

What you'll find in the book:

- how freezer meals can save you time and money
- making the most of your freezer space
- thawing your meals
- cooking tips for preparing and serving
- an essential what to stock in your freezer list
- best and worst ingredients to freeze
- how to freeze meats
- choosing your freezer containers
- sample one-week freezer meal plan
- Freezer recipes for breakfast
- freezer meals for lunch and dinner
- Freezer to crockpot meals
- Freezing condiments
- Freezing bread and bread dough
- Tips for using bread dough

- Soups to freeze
- Stock your Freezer with desserts
- Freezer Meal FAQ's
-

This book includes over 100 recipes as well as tips and tricks for great freezer meals, so you can be sure of delicious family-friendly results every time.

Save money with DIY convenience meals

When there are so many frozen convenience meals available for purchase at the supermarket, you might wonder if it is worth the extra effort making your own. It is! Most convenience meals only provide servings for one or two people, and there are no back-up options if you're still hungry once it's finished. As convenience meals do not have the same level of nutrients as fresh food, you are more likely to still be craving nourishment after dinner.

You can make your own marinated lamb or seasoned chicken breasts for a fraction of the "convenience" meal price. Buy a bulk portion of meat and separate it into smaller portions yourself. Slice or shred the meat, add your own seasoning or marinade, place the meat in labeled plastic freezer bags, and voila! Your home-made, cost-effective freezer meals are ready when you want them.

Organizing your time

You don't need to be daunted at the prospect of filling your freezer with readymade meals. There are a few practical ways to maintain your supply of freezer meals without making it into a chore.

- When you are making pasta sauce, soup or some other meal that would freeze well, make double or triple the required amount, so you can pack one or two extra meals into the freezer without any extra effort.

- Once a month, set aside a day for making bulk portions of your family's favorite freezer meals.

- Only make bulk portions of freezer meals that are guaranteed family favorites. You don't want to waste valuable freezer space on a meal that nobody wants to defrost. If you're not sure whether a certain meal will work well as a freezer meal, have a practice run of one family-size freezer meal. If it is popular, you can make a larger quantity next time.

- Work out how many freezer meals you will need each week and you will have a better idea of how many spare meals you need to keep in your freezer. For example, if Monday and Thursday afternoons are crammed with after-school activities, you will appreciate pulling a filling and familiar meal from the freezer when you get home at dinner time; add one extra meal to cover an unusually busy day, and you will need to calculate on eating two or three freezer meals a week. Other nights, you can eat freshly cooked meals, and maybe even stock up your freezer at the same time!

Making the most of your freezer space

Before you start stocking up your freezer, you need to assess how you can use the space efficiently. Otherwise you will come home from shopping with several bulk packs of meat and vegetables and find that the freezer is already full. If you repeatedly pull out all the items to re-sort them, you are risking freezer burn, so you need an efficient and flexible system.

Plastic "sheet" storage for small freezers

If you only have a small freezer, try packing your meals in plastic freezer bags. Arrange the food into a flat "sheet" for easy storage, and make sure you remove all the air from the bag before sealing it. You can stack 5-10 of these frozen "sheets" in your freezer.

For soups and marinated meats, seal the bag carefully to prevent leakage. You can use two bags for extra protection.

Delegate containers

It is easier to keep track of your stored goods if you have specific containers for different frozen items. Sturdy square or rectangular containers are easier to shuffle around when you need to re-sort the items in your freezer. The best containers have thick walls to stand up to the pressure of packing, and locking lids to prevent freezer burn.

Removable Shelves

Purchase simple plastic shelving from your local hardware or general store so you can slot in an extra row of containers. This way, you are not stacking containers on top of each other and you increase the natural airflow around the frozen food, so your freezer doesn't have to work so hard.

Clean out regularly

It is tempting to quickly freeze a left-over item, telling yourself you will use it later. But those forgotten odds and ends soon stack up, so make a rule to clear out your freezer regularly so you can make an inventory of what is available. This is your opportunity to find a use for the left-over banana pulp or thaw out the chicken casserole that has already been stored for long enough. You can also rearrange items so the older freezer meals are prominently at the front.

While you are clearing out, you can also remove built-up ice and wipe down the shelves thoroughly. A clean freezer works more efficiently and you will find it easier to locate the right meal for the next occasion.

Thawing your meals

The best way to thaw your meals is to take the chosen meal out of the freezer the night before and allow it to thaw in a dish in the fridge. By the time you're ready to prepare dinner, you can easily heat the thawed meal in the microwave, the oven or over the stove.

If you are unexpectedly drawing on your freezer meal supply, you can thaw the freezer meal in the microwave.

Cooking tips for preparing and serving perfect freezer meals

o A good test of whether an item is suitable for freezing is to ask yourself how the item will taste with extra water content. When you thaw any food, its water content increases. Soups are ideal for freezing, as the extra water content is unnoticed. Raw meats can be thawed slowly and then cooked, evaporating the water content. But milk products and some fruits will lose their texture and flavor when overloaded with water.

o Most vegetables freeze well, and they will thaw well alongside meat if you chop them well when adding them to the meal. This also ensures your freezer meal is a balanced meal with plenty of healthy nutrients.

o Keep a supply of frozen bread rolls or home-made garlic bread in the freezer, so you can serve these alongside your freezer meals.

o Potatoes do not freeze well on their own, so if you want to have potatoes with your freezer meal, it is usually best to cook them separately on the day. However, potatoes can be successfully frozen when they are thoroughly incorporated within a moist or liquid meal, such as a casserole.

o When you are preparing cooked meals such as lasagna or casseroles for the freezer, slightly undercook the meal. It will make up the cooking time during the thawing and reheating process.

o Sour cream does not freeze or thaw well, so if your recipe calls for a spoonful of sour cream, add this when you thaw and heat the recipe before serving.

o Rice, pasta and other noodles are also best cooked fresh to serve alongside your freezer meal.

o Don't confine yourself to family dinners. You can also freeze cakes, muffins and cookies for snacks, and you can even freeze waffles and pancakes for an easy and luxurious breakfast.

o After cooking your latest batch of meals for the freezer, allow the meal to cool at room temperature for 30-45 minutes before placing the meals into the freezer.

o You can freeze uncooked casseroles. Allow for 1-hour cooking time after thawing.

o Freeze some meals in individual servings and other meals in family-size servings, so you are ready for anything! These individual meals can be used for packed lunches.

o Label your freezer meals clearly and with plenty of detail. It's important to know whether the apricot chicken is pre-cooked or has been marinated raw! It also helps to write the date of freezing, so you can be sure to eat the oldest meals first, and keep your supplies fresh and up to date.

o Make up a code for your freezer labels so you know whether the meal requires freshly cooked potatoes/ rice/ pasta; whether it is raw or precooked, and what thawing/ cooking time it requires; whether it should be topped with cheese; serving size; and whether it includes vegetables.

o Organize your freezer meals so the new meals are placed at the bottom of the stack, so the older meals are at the top for easy access.

o Keep a supply of frozen grated cheese in the freezer, so you can top dishes such as lasagna with an extra layer of cheese before re-heating.

o If you are placing a freezer meal directly into the oven, increase the cooking time as it will need to thaw before cooking and heating.

Best choice freezer meals

Once you adjust to the routine of freezer meals, you will look beyond the basic Bolognese sauce for dinner and consider how you can prepare breakfasts, lunches and snacks to have on hand.

Breakfast

Pancakes and waffles are both great to have stored in the freezer. Cook up a batch of toaster-size pancakes or waffles, then freeze them individually on a baking tray. Once they are frozen, place a stack into a large Ziploc bag. To thaw and cook, place each pancake/ waffle into the toaster. Serve with a drizzle of syrup and fresh fruit.

Another classic breakfast option is sausage or bacon, cooked in advance and then frozen. When cooking, leave the bacon or sausage slightly under-done, so the remaining cooking time can be completed as part of the thawing and reheating process.

Lunch

With a little foresight, you can have some versatile and tasty lunch ingredients on hand. Stock up on burritos, which should be cooked in advance so you can reheat and serve. Other foods, like home-made pizzas can be assembled then frozen uncooked. Pizzas thaw and cook quickly, and they make a great standby when you have a few extra people over for a casual lunch.

Dinner

Dinners are the most popular meals to store in the freezer, whether cooked in advance or uncooked. Casseroles, soups and some pies can be cooked and frozen, while pasta dishes like lasagna can be frozen while they are partially cooked.

Crock pot Freezer Meals

The crock pot is a fantastic time-saving kitchen appliance, as you can throw all your dinner ingredients into the pot in the morning, and a perfectly cooked meal will emerge that evening. You can save even more time by doubling your quantities and freezing one crock pot meal to eat on another day. Alternately you can also bulk-cook large chunks of meat such as pork, brisket, beef, lamb, chicken and ribs are all ideal for crock pot cooking, once you add some stock and flavoring to make a great sauce. If your meal requires soft vegetables (such as fresh beans) or potatoes, it is best to add these before serving, rather than freezing them along with the crock pot meal. Soft vegetables are better when they are only cooked for a short time in relation to other crock pot ingredients, while potatoes lose their texture when they are frozen.

However, if you want to save yourself cooking with a freezer meal that requires potatoes, try cooking the potatoes in the crock pot. Wash and scrub the potatoes in the morning, and rub the skins with butter or oil. Place them in the crock pot and cook on low throughout the day. Serve with your casserole freezer meal and some freshly cooked beans (which should only take a few minutes). Soups are also excellent freezer meals and they are easy to make in the crock pot. You can also try freezing your soup ingredients and store them in a bag to unthaw and pour straight into the crock pot. As soup is a fluid meal, the excess moisture accumulated through freezing and thawing does not affect the final outcome.

You'll find some crockpot freezer recipes later in the book.

Essential freezer food list

Some of these items might not seem like freezer foods, but they are great to have on hand and freezing helps them last longer and stay fresher.

Raw meat: chicken breasts, ground beef, roast chicken
Broth or stocks
Pre-cooked ground hamburger to use in soups, tacos, or taco salads.
Pre-cooked shredded chicken for soups, chicken salads, sandwiches, casseroles.
Frozen vegetables- broccoli, cauliflower, spinach, carrots, mixed
Frozen fruit, variety
Bread dough
Bread rolls
Loaves of bread
Bread crumbs
Tortillas
Pie shells
Chocolate chips
Nuts
Yeast
Butter
Frozen juices

Best – and worst - ingredients for freezing

Some foods freeze better than others. The relative success of a meal or ingredient depends on the water content – the higher the water content of a food, the lower the freezing quality. Fried foods also do not freeze well, as they lose their characteristic crispness at some point during the freezing and thawing process.

Meats

Meats freeze well because they are so dense and there are few places for air to hide. Pre-cooked meats do not freeze so well, unless they are frozen along with a sauce – for example, as Bolognese sauce or as a casserole.

Fruits and Vegetables

When vegetables are frozen at their peak freshness, they retain this freshness and all their nutrients. To freeze your own vegetables, blanch them in boiling water for 1-2 minutes to preserve the bright natural color, then drain them and allow them to cool before freezing in air tight bags. Pack the vegetables carefully so the individual vegetables do not freeze into one unappetizing block. One strategy is to place the vegetables on flat cookie sheets, so they don't touch each other and then partially freezing them before packing them together in air-tight bags. This is called flash freezing.

How to freeze meats

Meat is probably the most expensive food product you purchase, and you can save money by bulk-buying and freezing the excess. However, your frugality will be wasted if the meat goes bad due to poor packing and freezing.

Preparing to freeze meats

Slice or chop the meat and divide into serving-size portions before freezing, so you only need to thaw the meat you intend to cook immediately. Smaller portions of meat will also freeze more quickly and successfully. It is best to cut the meat into individual portions before freezing because the meat could spoil if it has to be thawed and reheated numerous times.

Once the meat is cut and divided, wrap each portion in thick plastic wrap and place in an airtight container. Return the meat to the fridge to ensure it returns to a chilled temperature before transferring to the freezer. Raw meat should always be chilled at 40° F (4°C) to prevent bacteria multiplying. Chilled meat also freezes more quickly, minimizing the development of ice crystals.

Monitor the freezer temperature

Your freezer should be consistently set between 0 and -10 °F (-18 to -23°C) to ensure your frozen goods stay fully frozen. When your freezer is set to the correct temperature, your meat will freeze faster and will develop smaller ice crystals. If your freezer is empty, turn it down to -10 °F (-23°C) the day before you intend to freeze meat. This will help the meat freeze more quickly. Once the freezer is full, you can count on the frozen goods to maintain a consistent temperature, so you can raise the freezer temperature to closer than 0 °F (-18 °C).

Positioning meat in the freezer

Frozen meat should be stored at the bottom of the freezer.
The cold air radiating from the other frozen goods will help
keep the meat frozen, so the freezer does not need to exert so
much power to maintain temperature. Remember, meat
should never be thawed and re-frozen, as this will lead to
serious oxidation and freezer burn.

Choosing your freezer containers

The right freezer containers will not only help you protect your freezer meals from freezer burn, they can also make it easier to stack and sort your freezer. As an added advantage, a good container can be used repeatedly, saving money and waste in the long-term. Containers do not have to be expensive to be good quality, so long as you know what you need. So, what should you look for in a freezer container?

A variety of sizes
With a range of sizes, you can pack your freezer more efficiently and you will always have the right size container for each meal. When you fill a container up to the top, there is less room for air inside the container, lowering the risk of oxidization.

Air tight seals
Your container needs a firm locking system and a rubber gasket to seal out air and moisture, so you can keep the contents fresh for longer.

Good writing surface
You want to either be able to repeatedly write and erase on your containers so you always have up-to-date labels on your freezer meals. If the surface is not good for writing on, try stick-on labels or a streak of chalk-board paint for writing on.

Stacking ability
Make sure your containers have flat lids and compatible shapes so they can fit neatly together and stack securely. It is now possible to buy containers with locking lids, so they will stack more safely. This will help keep your freezer neat

and easy to negotiate as you find the right freezer meal for the next occasion.

Freezer Meals One-Week Meal Plan

If you have a hectic week coming up, you can stock up in advance so all your dinners are available from the freezer. As a bonus, you can keep a stock of bread rolls and a pizza crust in the freezer for lunch each day.

Day 1 – Spaghetti Bolognese
Preparation: make Bolognese sauce and freeze in an air-tight container.
On the day: In the morning, take sauce out of freezer and leave to thaw in the fridge. In the evening, heat the sauce in a saucepan and make pasta.

Day 2 – Slow-Cook Lemon & Lime Chicken
Preparation: Place 8 chicken drumsticks in a ziplock bag. In a jug, mix 1/2 cup chicken broth with 2 tablespoons lemon juice, 2 tablespoons lime juice, 2 cloves minced garlic, 1 teaspoon parsley, 1 teaspoon oregano, a pinch of salt and pepper. Pour the mixture over the chicken in the ziplock bag. Seal, double bag and freeze.
The night before: remove the bag out of the freezer and leave to thaw in the fridge.
On the day: Place the contents into the crock pot. Cook for 6-8 hours on low. Serve with rice and steamed vegetables.

Day 3 – Soup with bread rolls
Preparation: Make your favorite soup recipe. Cool the soup, then place into an air-tight container. Place some bread rolls in a plastic bag. The night before: Remove the soup from the freezer and leave to thaw in the fridge.
On the day: Place the thawed contents into a saucepan and heat gently. Remove the bread roll from the freezer and leave to thaw at room temperature.

Day 4 - Meatloaf

Preparation: Make your favorite meatloaf recipe. Line a loaf pan with foil, leaving overlapping edges over the sides. Flash freeze the meatloaf, then lift it out of the tin using the foil overlap as handles. Wrap completely in tin foil and freeze.

On the day: Remove from freezer and place in original loaf pan. Bake at 375° F (190°C) for one hour.

Day 5 – Pork Chop Casserole

Preparation: Place 3 pounds (1 kg) pork chops in a casserole dish. Mix 1/2 cup honey, 1/4 cup soy sauce, 2 tbsp. basil, 2 tbsp. garlic, 2 tbsp. oregano, 2 tbsp. olive oil in a jug and pour over pork chops. Cook on medium low for two hours. Cool before freezing in an air-tight container.

The night before: Remove from freezer and leave to thaw in the refrigerator. On the day: Heat the casserole in a saucepan. Serve with potatoes and fresh vegetables.

Day 6 -Taco Kits

Preparation: Mix cooked ground hamburger with refried beans. Season with taco seasoning and 1/2 Cup salsa. Cool before freezing in an air-tight container.

On the day: Thaw in the microwave. Serve with tortillas, shredded lettuce, shredded cheese and taco sauce.

Day 7 – Ham and onion quiche

Preparation: Thaw a sheet of frozen pastry and press it into a foil pie pan. Place an even layer of chopped ham and diced onion over the pastry. Beat together 6 eggs, 1 cup milk, salt and pepper in a mixing bowl. Cook until just firm and allow to cool. Wrap in foil and place in a zip-lock bag.

On the day: In the morning, remove quiche from freezer and place in refrigerator. To cook, remove from bag and place foil pan in oven. Bake at 375° F (190°C) for 40 minutes or until heated through and golden on top.

Freezer Recipes

Breakfast Meals

Frozen Waffles from a Box

Ingredients

2 cups packaged pancake waffle mix
wax paper, cut into squares slightly larger than waffles
Freezer wrap

Method

Prepare waffles as directed on the package. Pour about 1/2 cup of batter into a preheated waffle iron. Cook according to waffle iron directions, then remove waffle and cool on wire rack. Continue until you have used up the waffle batter.

Once the waffles have cooled, place a sheet of waxed paper on the counter. Place one waffle on the wax paper, then top with another sheet of wax paper. Stack all the waffles in this fashion. Wrap the stack tightly in freezer wrap. Freeze for up to 2 months.

Reheat waffles in a toaster on low setting or place in an oven preheated to 450 °F (230°C) and bake for 3 to 5 minutes or until heated through.

You can also place waffles in an oven to reheat. Preheat oven to 450 degrees.

Place then directly on the oven rack and bake 3 to 5 minutes or until heated through.

Ham and Hash Brown Rollups

Ingredients

1 tbsp. olive oil
1 ham steak, cut into pieces
2 cups frozen southern style hash browns, thawed
8 eggs
1/2 cup salsa
6 tortillas
1 cup shredded cheese
wax paper
freezer bags

Method

In a skillet, heat olive oil and cook ham and hash browns until they start to brown.
Place the salsa and eggs in a large mixing bowl and stir until well combined. Pour the salsa mixture into skillet with the ham mixture and cook at medium high until the eggs have set.
Place 4 tablespoons of the ham mixture down the center of a flat tortilla. Roll the tortilla up completely. Continue until all the tortillas are used. Wrap each rollup in wax paper.
Place in a freezer bag and freeze for up to 2 months.
When ready to eat remove from the freezer and unwrap. Place each rollup on a microwave safe plate and cover with paper towel. Microwave 2 minutes on high or until the burrito is heated through.

French Toast Sticks

Ingredients
2 eggs, lightly beaten
4 tablespoons milk
1 teaspoon cinnamon
Bread, sliced

Method
Beat eggs, cinnamon and milk in a flat dish. Heat griddle. Dip both sides of bread into egg mixture and place bread on griddle. Cook until each side is browned. Cut each slice into three rectangles. Allow to cool and place on a cookie sheet to flash freeze. Place French toast sticks in a freezer bag.
When ready to eat, warm French toast sticks in microwave and serve with syrup.

Spiced Pumpkin Muffins

Ingredients
1/2 cup of sugar
1/2 cup light brown sugar, packed
6 tbsp. unsalted butter, room temperature
2 tsp cinnamon
1 1/2 tsp ground ginger
1/2 tsp ground cloves 1 tsp baking powder
1 tsp baking soda
3/4 tsp salt
2 tsp vanilla extract
2 large eggs
2 large egg whites
1 1/4 Cups canned pumpkin
2 1/2 Cups of whole white-wheat flour
1/2 Cup of milk

Method
Preheat oven to 350°F (180°C). Line 20 muffin tin cups with paper liners. Place the white sugar, brown sugar and butter in a mixing bowl. Add spices, baking powder, salt and vanilla. Beat with hand mixer on medium speed until just blended. Add the whole eggs and egg whites one at a time, beating well after each addition Add the pumpkin and beat in on low speed until just blended in. Add the flour 1/3 at a time and alternate with the milk half at a time, beating until just combined. Using an ice cream scoop, fill each cup about 2/3 full. Bake the muffins for 30 minutes or until a toothpick inserted in the center comes out clean. Cool for 5 minutes in the pan then remove to a wire rack to continue cooling.

Place muffins in a Ziploc bag and freeze. Thaw overnight before serving.

Heat & Eat Pancakes

Ingredients

2 1/2 cups milk
2 eggs
1/3 cup canola oil
1 tablespoon of vanilla
1/4 tsp salt
1/2 cup sugar
1/2 cup wheat flour
4 tsp baking powder
Extra all-purpose flour to thicken batter as required
Wax paper cut into squares slightly larger than your intended pancake
Freezer bags

Method

Whisk the milk, eggs, oil and vanilla into a large mixing bowl until just blended together. Add the salt and sugar and beat until smooth. Add the wheat flour and baking powder. Beat until smooth.

Add just enough all-purpose flour to thicken batter to your liking. Heat a griddle over medium high heat. Pour about 1/2 cup of batter onto hot griddle.

Cook until pancake begins to bubble and edges lift. Flip and cook about 2 minutes or until both sides are lightly brown. Continue cooking until all the batter is used.

Cool pancakes completely and then place a pancake on one sheet of wax paper. Place another sheet of wax paper on top of the pancake. Continue stacking pancakes and wax paper until all the pancakes are used.

Place into a freezer bag and freeze up to 6 months. To reheat, just drop into the toaster. Toast 2 cycles if necessary.

Classic Pancake Recipe

Ingredients

3 eggs
1 cup milk
1 1/2 cups flour
1/2 tsp salt
3 tablespoons vegetable oil
3 teaspoons baking powder
1 tablespoon sugar

Method

In mixing bowl add all ingredients and blend together.
Heat griddle and cook pancakes flipping over after pancakes bubble. Allow to cool and place in between sheets of
waxed paper. Freeze in freezer bag. When ready to eat
place in toaster.

Bacon & Egg Cupcakes

Ingredients

3 Tablespoons butter
2 cups mushrooms, sliced
1 cup diced bacon
2 Cups broccoli flowerets
2 Tablespoons olive oil
1 Cup cheese, grated
Salt and pepper
9 large eggs

Method

Preheat oven to 350°F (180°C). Place paper cups in cup cake pan. In a skillet, melt butter and sauté mushrooms and bacon. Chop the mushrooms and steam broccoli 5-7 minutes.

In a bowl, add broccoli and olive oil and mash with a fork until chunky. Add mushrooms and grated cheese. Season with salt and pepper.

In a jug, beat eggs and a splash of water until light and fluffy.

Fill each cupcake half full of vegetable and bacon mixture. Pour egg mixture over vegetables in cupcake tins. Bake 10 minutes. Allow to cool, then wrap each cupcake in plastic wrap and store in refrigerate or freezer.

When ready to eat, warm up in microwave.

Lunch and Dinner Recipes

Chicken Stock or Broth

Chicken stock is a great standby as a base for casserole and crock-pot meals. You can improvise with a variation of ingredients at hand to achieve your own individual flavor.

Method

Place roast chicken in a large soup pot with chopped carrots, a quartered onion, 1-2 celery leaves and 2 bay leaves. Cover with water and bring to a boil. Simmer on medium-low 1 hour and then drain broth into a freezer container. Allow to cool.

Shred chicken and set aside for a casserole or other dish. Once the broth has cooled, store in freezer.

Homemade Spaghetti Sauce

Ingredients
2 Tablespoon olive oil
1 onion, chopped
1 garlic clove, crushed
1 teaspoon Italian seasoning
1/4 teaspoon cayenne pepper
1 pound (500g) minced beef
5 cups tomatoes, chopped and pureed
1/4 cup ketchup
2 teaspoon Worcestershire sauce
2 teaspoon dried oregano
1 cup beef or vegetable stock
salt and pepper

Method
Sauté onion and garlic in olive oil, and add herbs and cayenne. Add beef and cook until browned. Set aside. Pour tomatoes, ketchup, Worcestershire sauce, oregano, stock and seasonings into a large soup pot. Cover pot and simmer for at least 30 minutes. Add beef and combine well. Remove from heat and allow to cool completely. Freeze in desired proportions.

Classic Meatloaf or Meatballs

Ingredients

2 eggs
1 cup milk
1/2 cup dry bread crumbs
3 teaspoon seasoning salt
1 tbsp. Worcestershire sauce
1/2 tsp pepper
2 lb. (900g) ground hamburger

Method

Place all ingredients together in bowl and combine, using your hands. For loaves, shape mixture into loaves and place each loaf in disposable foil loaf pans. Wrap loaf pans in foil and freeze. To serve, place frozen meatloaf in oven at and bake at 350 ° F (180 ℃) for 1 hour -1 1/2 hours.

For meatballs, use the above recipe and shape the mixture into small balls. Place each meatball in a lined or greased cupcake tray and cook at 350 ° F (180 ℃) for 13-20 minutes until cooked through. Once cooled, flash freeze then store in freezer bag. To serve, warm up meatballs in oven or microwave.

~Use meatballs in a variety of recipes such as sweet and sour meatballs, spaghetti, meatball sandwiches, etc.

Mini Calzones

Ingredients
pizza dough - store bought or homemade
8 oz. (225g) mozzarella cheese, cubed
Pepperoni, sliced
Ham, diced
1/4 cup olive oil
1 tsp dried Italian seasoning
3 tbsp. grated Parmesan cheese

Method
Roll pizza dough onto a floured surface and roll into a large rectangle. Cut into squares, approx. 4 inches across. Top each square with pepperoni, ham and cheese. Wrap dough around meat, fold sides in and roll up. Press edges together. Place the calzones on a lined cookie sheet.
In a small bowl, mix olive oil and seasoning. Using a pastry brush, brush oil over calzones. Bake at 400° F (205°C) for 15 minutes. Allow to cool then flash freeze, then place in one container to freeze together. After thawing, sprinkle with Parmesan cheese and bake at 400° F (205°C) for 8 minutes to heat through.
Serve with tomato sauce.

Enchilada Filling

Ingredients

4 cups shredded chicken
8 oz. (225g) cream cheese, softened
1/2 cup salsa
1 cup shredded cheddar cheese
1 can cream of chicken soup
1 cup of milk
salt and pepper
To serve: enchiladas, salsa and shredded cheese

Method

Stir chicken and cream cheese in bowl. Add
seasoning to taste. In separate bowl mix 1-2 cans of
cream of chicken soup (depending on how much you
are making) and 1 cup milk. Depending on the desired
consistency of your filling, add 1/2 cup to 1 cup of
soup mixture to chicken mixture. Combine well.
Freeze enchilada filling in an air-tight container.
Freeze remaining soup mixture to use as sauce.
To serve, remove container of chicken and container
of sauce from freezer, and thaw at room temperature
overnight. Spoon chicken mixture down center of
each tortilla and roll up. Place seam side down in
greased baking dish. Pour sauce mixture over top and
top with shredded cheese and salsa. Bake at 350 ° F
(180 ° C) degrees for 20 minutes.

Sloppy Joes

Ingredients
1 pound (500g) lean ground beef
1 medium onion, chopped
1/4 cup chopped celery
1-2 carrots
1 green pepper chopped
1 cup ketchup
1 tbsp. Worcestershire sauce
1 tbsp. brown sugar
1 tsp yellow mustard
1/8 teaspoon black pepper

Method
Puree onion, celery, carrots and pepper in blender. Sauté beef and vegetable puree in pan until beef is browned. Add ketchup, Worcestershire sauce, brown sugar, mustard and pepper. Simmer for 10 minutes. Cool and place in foil container. Wrap in foil and place in air-tight bag.

To serve, remove from freezer and thaw for 12 hours in the refrigerator. Bake in oven at 350 ° F (180 ° C) for 50-60 minutes or until heated through. Sprinkle with grated cheese and return to oven until cheese has melted. Serve with mashed potatoes and fresh vegetables.

Manicotti with cheese filling

Manicotti and lasagna are two of the few pastas that freeze well. Bake until almost done before freezing so you can complete the baking process when you heat the thawed meal.

Ingredients

1 box manicotti noodles
8 oz. (225g) mozzarella cheese
2 cup cottage cheese
3/4 cup grated parmesan cheese
2 tbsp. parsley
l egg, beaten
1/2 tsp Salt
1/2 tsp Pepper
1 jar of spaghetti sauce

Method

Cook manicotti noodles and rinse in cold water. In separate bowl, mix cheeses, egg and parsley together. Stuff noodles with cheese mixture.

Line baking pan with foil, with plenty of foil overlapping the sides. Pour 1/2 spaghetti sauce in bottom of baking pan. Place noodles on top and pour remaining sauce over noodles. Cover with foil and cook at 350 ° F (180 ° C) for 35 minutes covered with foil. Allow to cool then remove from pan by lifting overlapping foil. Place in an air-tight container and freeze.

To serve, thaw for 12 hours in refrigerator, then bake for 20 minutes. Serve with fresh salad and garlic bread.

Chicken Roll Ups

Ingredients

Filling
2 cups chicken cooked and shredded
8 ounces cream cheese
Salt and pepper
Crescent roll dough
Broth sauce
2 Tablespoons Parsley
2 Cups chicken broth
2 Tablespoons cornstarch
pinch pepper

Method

For filling, mix chicken and cheese, then season to taste.
Roll dough out and separate into triangles. Place a
spoonful of filling on dough and roll up. Flash freeze
before storing in air-tight container. To serve, thaw for
12 hours in refrigerator then bake at 350 ° F (180 ° C)
for 15 minutes until golden and crisp. Serve with broth
sauce.
To make broth sauce, combine ingredients in a saucepan
and heat for several minutes until thickened slightly.
Allow to cool then store in freezer in an air-tight
container.

Swiss Meatballs

Ingredients
1/2 lb. (225g) ground beef
1/2 lb. (225g) ground pork
1 1/2 cup shredded Swiss cheese, divided
1 egg, slightly beaten
1 small onion, chopped
1 tsp celery salt
1/4 tsp nutmeg
1/4 tsp allspice
3 cups cooked rice, divided
1 (10 oz.) can cream of mushroom soup
3/4 cup milk
3 garlic cloves, minced
1/2 cup grated Parmesan cheese

Method
Place the ground meats into a large mixing bowl and add the egg, onion and seasonings. Sprinkle in 1/2 cup of Swiss cheese and 1 cup of the cooked rice. Mix well using your hands. Mold into meatballs then place meatballs in large baking dish and bake for 25 minutes at 350 ° F (180 ° C). Cool.

Meanwhile combine remaining Swiss cheese, remaining rice soup, milk, garlic and Parmesan cheese. Mix well.

Line a baking dish with foil, ensuring the foil overlaps generously. Pour the Swiss cheese mixture into the baking dish and add the cooked meatballs. Cover with freezer wrap and freeze for up to 3 months.

To serve, thaw casserole in refrigerator for 12 hours. Bake for 45 minutes at 350 ° F (180 ° C).

Homemade chicken nuggets

Ingredients

1 egg
1/2 Cup Parmesan cheese
1/4 Cup dry bread crumbs
1 teaspoon oregano and parsley
1/4 teaspoon paprika
salt and pepper
4-5 chicken breasts, cut in strips

Method

Beat egg lightly in a shallow bowl. In a second bowl, mix cheese, bread crumbs and seasonings. Dip chicken in beaten egg and coat with crumb mixture. Bake at 400 degrees for 20-25 minutes. Flash freeze and store in an air-tight container.
To serve, thaw in refrigerator for 12 hours then bake at 400°F (205°C) for 10 minutes or until heated through and serve with selection of sauces.

~Double the recipe if you'd like to store more.

Pizza Empandas

Ingredients
1 1/2 cups flour
1 cup cornmeal
1tsp baking powder
1/4 tsp salt
1 tsp sugar
1/3 cup butter, softened
1/2 cup milk
1 cup pizza sauce
1/2 cup shredded cheese

Method
Combine dry ingredients with butter in mixer. Gradually add milk until the dough is firm and can be shaped into a ball. If dough becomes sticky, finish adding milk and add more cornmeal.
Place half the dough on a floured surface and roll out until 1/8 inch thick. Cut into circles about 3-4 inch in diameter. Combine sauce and cheese in a small bowl and place 1 tsp. of mixture onto every circle. Fold each circle in half and seal with fork along edges. Bake at 400°F (205°C) on ungreased baking sheet for 12 minutes. Allow to cool then flash freeze, then freeze in air tight container.
To serve, thaw for 12 hours and heat in oven.

Glazed Ham Loaf

Ingredients

Ham loaf
1 cup cracker crumbs
3 eggs, beaten
1/4 tsp pepper
1 1/2 lb. (700 g) ground ham
1 1/2 lb. (700g) ground pork or sausage

Glaze
1 cup brown sugar
1 teaspoon mustard
1/4 cup vinegar
1/4 cup water

Method

To make loaf, combine ingredients and blend well. Shape into a loaf. Place into a disposable aluminum loaf pan. (Depending on size of loaf pan, you could make two loaves. Alternately, you can use any excess loaf mixture to make meatballs.)

To make ham glaze, mix all ingredients in a jug and pour over ham loaf. Wrap loaf pan in tin foil and freeze.

To serve, thaw for 12 hours then bake at 350 ° F (180 ° C) for 2 hours.

To make meatballs, shape loaf mixture into balls and flash freeze then store in one bag. Freeze ham glaze separately. Thaw and combine in casserole dish to cook.

Barbecue Meatballs

Ingredients

1 egg, beaten
1/3 cup milk
1/4 cup Barbecue sauce
1/4 cup crushed stuffing
1 tbsp. onion soup mix
1 1/4 lbs. (500g) ground beef

Method

Combine all ingredients together and shape into meatballs. Flash freeze on cookie sheet then store in a Ziploc bag. To cook, thaw for 12 hours in refrigerator, then cook at cook at 350 ° F (180 °C) for 30 minutes or until cooked through. Serve with dipping sauce and with toothpicks.

Instant Burgers

Ingredients
2 lb. (900 g) ground beef
Wax paper, cut into 4-inch squares
Freezer paper

Method
Shape the ground beef into four-inch diameter patties. Stack patties with a layer of wax paper between each one. Wrap each stack in freezer paper and secure tightly. Freeze for up to 2 months.
Thaw in refrigerator for 12 hours. To cook, heat oil in a skillet and add patties, cooking for 5 minutes on each side.

Cheesy Bacon Meatloaf

Ingredients

3 oz. (100g) diced bacon
1 egg, beaten
1/3 cup crackers crushed
5 tbsp. shredded Swiss cheese
1/2 onion, finely chopped
1 garlic clove, minced
Salt and pepper to taste
1/2 lb. (225g) ground beef

Method

Combine egg, crackers, 4 tbsp. cheese, onion, garlic, bacon, salt and
pepper. Add beef into mixture and combine. Shape into loaf and freeze in a disposable foil loaf pan wrapped in foil.
To cook, remove from freezer and remove foil wrapping. Place loaf pan in oven and cook at 350 ° F (180 °C) for 30 minutes to 1 hour.
Serve with ketchup or barbeque sauce.

Pepperoni Pasta Bake

Ingredients

1 lb. (500g) ground beef
1 medium onion, chopped
1 small green pepper, chopped
4 oz. (100g) mushrooms, chopped
26 oz. (730g) jar pasta sauce
8 oz. (200g) tomato sauce
1 tsp Italian seasoning
1 lb. (500g) spiral or shell pasta
3/4 cups milk
2 eggs, slightly beaten
5 oz. (140g) sliced pepperoni
1 1/2 cup shredded Cheddar cheese
2 cup shredded Monterey Jack cheese

Method

Drain and rinse. Place ground beef in a large skillet over medium high heat. Add the onion, green pepper and mushrooms. Cook until meat is browned being sure to crumble the meat. Drain. Add the pasta sauce, tomato sauce and Italian seasoning. Stir until well combined. Simmer for 15 minutes. Place the eggs and milk in a large bowl and blend. Place the pasta in the egg mixture and toss to cover. While sauce is simmering, cook pasta as directed on the package. Place half of the pasta mixture into the bottom of a disposable foil pan. Place half of the meat sauce over the top of the spaghetti. Continue layering until all pasta and meat is finished. Cool the casserole in the refrigerator, then wrap with freezer wrap and freeze for up to 2 months. To serve, thaw for 12 hours in refrigerator. Cover with foil and bake at 350 ° F (180 °C) for 45 minutes. Remove foil and top casserole with pepperoni and cheese. Bake for 15 minutes or until cheese has melted and casserole is heated through.

Chicken Cordon Bleu

Ingredients

6 chicken breasts
6 slices Swiss cheese
6 slices ham
1 can cream of chicken soup
1/2-pint sour cream

Method

Beat chicken breast flat with meat tenderizer or rolling pin.
Slice chicken breast open to make a "pocket" and tuck
slice of ham and cheese in each pocket.
Blend soup and sour cream together. Pour sauce over
chicken.
Bake at 400°F (205°C) for 35-40 minutes. Allow to cool.
Wrap chicken breasts in foil and freeze.
To cook, unwrap chicken breast and place in casserole
dish. Bake 15-20 minutes at 350 ° F (180 °C). Serve with
steamed vegetables and rice.

Cheesy Spaghetti Bake

Ingredients

2 tbsp. melted butter
1 lb. (500g) mozzarella cheese
6 oz. (60g) spaghetti, cooked
2 eggs
1/2 Cup Parmesan cheese
1 large jar spaghetti sauce
8 oz. (225g) cottage cheese
1/2 lb. (250g) Hamburger
1 teaspoon oregano or Italian seasoning

Method

Mix butter and mozzarella, and toss through cooked pasta. Brown hamburger and drain off fat. Add spaghetti sauce and seasonings.

Pour noodle mixture into disposable foil baking pan. Top with parmesan cheese, cottage cheese, hamburger, mozzarella cheese and spaghetti

sauce. Bake at 350 ° F (180 ºC) for 25 minutes. Cool and wrap in tin foil. Freeze. To serve, place frozen spaghetti bake in oven and bake at 350 ° F (180 ºC) until heated through.

Mini-Freeze Pizzas

Ingredients

(Quantities calculated by the number of mini pizzas you want to make)

For base

English muffin, bagel or round bread roll, sliced in half

For topping

Pizza sauce, tomato sauce or spaghetti sauce

shredded mozzarella cheese

pepperoni, ham, sliced olives, mushrooms, diced onion, green peppers, chopped

Method

Place base of choice on a cookie sheet.

Spread sauce over base, sprinkle with cheese and sprinkle topping of choice. Flash freeze on cookie sheet. Then place in ziploc freezer bag.

To serve, bake at 375°F (190°C) for about 20 minutes or until golden brown.

Crumbed Tuna Turnovers

Ingredients

2 cans tuna, drained and flaked
1/2 cup shredded cheddar cheese
1/3 cup mayonnaise
1/3 cup chopped pickles
1/8-1/4 teaspoon lemon pepper seasoning
2 sheets of puff pastry, cut into 5-inch circles
1 egg, beaten
1 1/4 cups fine breadcrumbs, seasoned to taste with salt and
pepper

Method

Combine tuna, cheese, mayonnaise, pickles and lemon
pepper. Spoon 2 tablespoons of tuna mixture onto one side
of each pastry circle. Fold dough over filling and press
edges to seal.
Beat egg in small bowl. Place seasoned breadcrumbs in
another bowl. Place egg and potato chips in separate
bowls. Dip turnovers in egg, then crumb. Place on
baking sheet and bake at 375ºF (190ºC) for 18-20 minutes or
until golden brown. Allow to cool, then flash freeze and
place in freezer bags.
To serve, re-heat in the microwave or oven.

Broccoli Bites
Ingredients
20 oz. broccoli, cooked and drained
2 cups seasoned stuffing
1 cup grated Parmesan cheese
6 eggs, lightly beaten
1/2 cup butter or margarine, softened
1/2 teaspoon salt
1/4 teaspoon pepper

Method
Add all ingredients together and mix well. Shape into 1 in balls. Place in greased baking pan. Bake at 350 ° F (180 ºC) for 10-12 minutes or until golden brown. Flash freeze and then freeze in a container.

To serve, thaw in refrigerator then bake at 350 ° F (180 ºC) until heated through.

Mediterranean Chicken Casserole

Ingredients

2 tbsp. flour

1 tsp paprika

4 boneless, skinless chicken breasts cut into 3/4 in. pieces

6 tbsp. canola oil

2 red onions, diced

6 garlic cloves, minced

1 1/2 lb. (700g) chickpeas

3/4 cups chicken broth

2 (14 oz.) cans diced tomatoes, drained well

1 1/4 lb. (500g) baby spinach leaves

1/2 tsp salt

1/4 tsp pepper

Method

In a bowl, toss flour with paprika to season and coat chicken pieces. Set aside.

Place the oil into a large skillet over medium heat. Add the onions and garlic and stir until softened. Add chicken and cook 5 minutes or until the chicken is browned.

Stir in the garlic and chickpeas and cook 1 minute. Pour the broth into the skillet and allow mixture bubble for 3 minutes. Add the tomatoes and bring the mixture to a boil. Reduce heat and simmer 15 minutes.

Add the spinach and cook for 3 minutes. Remove from the heat and stir in the salt and pepper.

Allow mixture to cool and pack into air-tight containers. Keep frozen for up to 3 months.

To serve, thaw for 12 hours in the refrigerator. Place chicken in a deep baking dish, cover and heat at 350 ° F (180 ºC) for 15 minutes or until heated through.

Chicken Vegetable Cobbler

Ingredients

2 tbsp. canola oil
6 boneless, skinless chicken breasts cut into pieces
1/2 tsp salt
1/4 tsp pepper
2 red onions, sliced thin
2 celery ribs, chopped
1 C chicken broth
4 carrots, chopped
3 C of vegetable broth
8 tbsp. flour
8 tbsp. cornmeal
2 tbsp. butter
1 tsp milk
1 egg yolk, beaten

Method

Heat half the oil in a cast iron pan. Season chicken breasts evenly with the salt and pepper and cook in pan over medium heat, turning frequently until browned. Remove the chicken and set aside. Preheat the oven to 350 ° F (180 °C). Place the remaining oil into the pan and stir in the onions. Cook on low for 6 minutes or until soft. Add the celery and cook for 5 minutes. Pour in the chicken broth, adjust the heat to medium and let the wine bubble for 3 minutes. Stir in the carrots.

Return the chicken to the pan and pour the broth over the top. Cook over low heat for 1 hour or until the chicken is fork tender.

Place the flour and cornmeal into a mixing bowl. Rub the butter into the mixture until the mixture resembles bread crumbs. Stir in the milk a little at a time until the mixture forms into a soft dough. Roll the dough into a ball and chill for 20 minutes. Flatten the chilled dough out on a

floured surface. Cut out 18 rounds of dough with a cookie cutter. Brush each round of dough with a little of the beaten egg yolk and place on top of the casserole.
Bake the casserole in the preheated oven for 30 minutes or until topping is cooked through. Cool, then freeze in air-tight container for up to 3 months. To serve, thaw casserole in refrigerator for 12 hours. Heat casserole in 350 ° F (180 °C) for 40 minutes or until heated through.

Crispy Chicken from the Freezer

Ingredients

2 1/2 lbs. (1kg) fryer chicken, cut up
3/4 cup sour cream
1 tbsp. lemon juice
1 tsp Worcestershire sauce
1 tsp celery salt
Salt, pepper and paprika to taste
2 cloves garlic, chopped fine
1 cup dry bread crumbs

Method

Preheat oven to 350 ° F (180 °C).
Blend sour cream and lemon juice in a small bowl. Stir in Worcestershire sauce until completely combined. Add the celery salt, salt, pepper, paprika and garlic and mix well. Place bread crumbs in a shallow bowl or on a plate.
Dip chicken pieces into the sour cream mixture then toss in the bread crumbs. Place crumbed chicken pieces in the baking pan. Bake 50 minutes or until chicken is crisp and brown.
Leave chicken to cool before removing from pan then wrap each piece in aluminum foil. Freeze for up to 2 months.
To serve, reheat chicken in foil, in oven at 450 ° F (230 °C) for 35 minutes. Remove foil and return to oven for 10 minutes.

Chicken Burritos

Ingredients

3 boneless chicken breasts
8 oz. (225 g) salsa
14 oz. (400g) refried beans
8 oz. (225g) shredded taco cheese
8 tortillas
Wax paper

Method

Place the chicken breasts in a large pan and cover with salsa. Add enough water to cover the chicken. Place over medium high heat. Bring to a boil. Reduce heat to low and simmer 15 minutes until cooked through.
Remove chicken from pot and cool, then shred. Return the shredded chicken to the pot. Return to a boil until liquid is reduced and thickened.
Place beans and chicken mixture onto each tortilla and sprinkle with cheese. Roll tortilla tightly and wrap each burrito in the wax paper. Freeze burritos in ziploc bags for up to 3 months.
To cook, remove wax paper and place burritos in microwave until just thawing. Place slightly thawed burritos on baking tray and bake in oven at 350 ° F (180 ºC)
12 minutes or until the burrito just begins to brown.

Chicken Pie

Ingredients

1 whole chicken
2 celery stalks, chopped
1 medium onion, chopped
1 tbsp. parsley
1 bay leaf
2 tsp salt
10 oz. baby carrots
10 oz. peas
6 oz. mushrooms
1 cup light cream
1/4 tsp nutmeg
1/4 tsp celery salt
1/8 tsp pepper
1/2 cup all-purpose flour
2 pie crusts
4 foil pans

Method

Fill a large pot with water and place over high heat.
Add chicken, celery, onion, parsley, bay leaf and salt.
Bring to a rapid boil and reduce heat. Cover the pot
and simmer for 2 hours. Allow the chicken to cool in
the pan, then remove from broth and cut all the meat
from the chicken bones. Set the meat aside.
Strain the broth, reserving 5 cups.
Place the chicken, vegetables and mushrooms in a
large bowl and stir to combine. Set aside.
Place flour in a small mixing bowl and gradually add
one cup of broth, stirring to make a smooth paste. Set
aside.
Place 4 cups of reserved broth into a saucepan, and add
cream, nutmeg, celery and seasoning. Bring broth to
the boil, then add paste. Reduce to low heat and

simmer for 2 minutes.

Pour the broth over the chicken mixture and allow to cool.

Line both pans with pie crust. Fill the crust with chicken mixture, then cover with remaining crust. Seal edges securely all around.

Wrap in freezer paper and freeze for up to 3 months.

To prepare, place each pie on a cookie sheet and cut a slit in the top to release steam. Bake for 40 minutes at 450 °F (230 °C).

Home-made Tomato Sauce

Ingredients

4 tbsp. olive oil
4 garlic cloves, minced
2 (28 oz.) cans tomatoes, chopped
2 tbsp. tomato paste
2 tsp oregano 2 bay leaves
1/2 tsp salt
1/4 tsp pepper
2 tsp pesto

Method

Heat oil in a pan over medium heat. Add garlic, stirring
constantly, then add tomatoes and tomato paste. Bring
the mixture to a boil then add oregano and bay leaves.
Season to taste and simmer the mixture for 25 minutes.
Remove from the heat and add pesto, stirring well.
Allow to cool before freezing.
To prepare, thaw in refrigerator for 6 hours.

Mustard and Fennel Pork Casserole

Ingredients

6 tbsp. of olive oil
2 onions, sliced
2 fennel bulbs, sliced
2 lb. (1kg) lean pork, cubed
6 garlic cloves, minced
2/3 cup dry white wine
2 tbsp. coarse grain mustard
1 tsp paprika
1 tbsp. fresh sage leaves, chopped
1 tbsp. fresh rosemary leaves, chopped
2 tbsp. flour
3 cup of milk
1 tsp salt
1/2 tsp pepper

Method

In a large pan, heat the oil over medium heat then stir in the onions and fennel, cooking until just beginning to soften. Add the pork pieces and cook 5 minutes or until no longer pink. Add garlic for 1 minute and stir to combine, then add the wine and mustard, stirring to blend in well. Bring to the boil for 3 minutes, then add paprika, sage, rosemary and flour stirring well. Pour in the milk, stirring to combine. Season to taste and simmer for 5 minutes. Cool completely before transferring to freezer containers. Freeze for up to 3 months.

To prepare, thaw for 12 hours in the refrigerator. Heat in pan over stove until warmed through.

Shepherd's Pie

Ingredients
1 lb. (450g) potatoes, peeled and sliced
1 tbsp. of butter
1 tsp salt
1/2 tsp pepper
3 tbsp. olive oil
3 onions, diced 3 carrots, diced
1 1/4 lbs. (600g) lean ground beef
2 garlic cloves, minced
2 tsp oregano
8 oz. (225g) tomatoes, diced
4 oz. (110g) pkg. frozen peas

Method
Boil the potatoes in water for 15 minutes or until very soft. Drain the potatoes and mash them with butter and seasoning. Set potatoes aside.

Heat oil in pan over medium heat and add the onions and carrots, cooking until soft. Add beef and cook until browned through. Stir in the garlic and oregano and cook 1 minute. Add the tomatoes and bring the mixture to a boil then stir in the peas and lower the heat. Simmer for 20 minutes.

Allow to cool then place beef in foil casserole dish. Top with mashed potato. Pack in air-tight bag and freeze for up to 6 months.

To prepare, thaw casserole in refrigerator then bake for 25 minutes at 350 ° F (180 °C).

Mushroom Chicken

Ingredients
1 1/2 tbsp. of butter
1 1/2 tbsp. of oil
1 onion, finely chopped
5 garlic cloves, minced
3 bacon strips, roughly chopped
1 tbsp. fresh thyme leaves
8 oz. (225g) button mushrooms
4 Cups chicken broth
1 1/2 lb. (700g) boneless chicken pieces, sliced
1/2 tsp salt
1/4 tsp pepper

Method
Melt butter in pan and stir oil in to blend. Add the onions and cook over low heat, stirring, until they begin to soften. Add the garlic and bacon pieces and cook for 5 minutes. Add the thyme and mushrooms and cook 2 minutes longer. Add chicken broth. Bring to the boil, and add chicken pieces. Season to taste, and simmer for 20 minutes or until chicken is cooked through. Cool before freezing in an airtight container.
To prepare, thaw chicken in refrigerator for 12 hours. Place in a casserole dish and cook for 25 minutes at 350 ° F (180 °C)

Tomato Eggplant Casserole

Ingredients

6 tbsp. olive oil
6 garlic cloves, minced
50 oz. (1.4 kg) diced tomatoes
2 tbsp. tomato paste
2 tsp oregano
1 tsp thyme
1/2 tsp salt
1/4 tsp pepper
3 eggplants, sliced
1 1/4 cup of Parmesan cheese, grated
12 oz. (340g) mozzarella cheese, shredded

Method

Heat 4 tbsp. of the oil in a saucepan over low heat. Stir in the garlic and cook for 30 seconds. Add tomatoes, tomato paste, oregano and thyme. Bring the mixture to a gentle boil. Remove the mixture from the heat and season to taste.

Brush the eggplant slices with the remaining oil. Cook the eggplant in a skillet over medium heat for 3 minutes per side or until nicely browned.

Cover the base of a disposable foil pan with tomato sauce. Layer the eggplant slices over the sauce. Sprinkle evenly with Parmesan cheese. Continue layering eggplant and tomato sauce, finishing with tomato sauce. Sprinkle a thick layer of mozzarella cheese over the top. Cool and wrap tightly before storing in the freezer. Freeze for up to 3 months.

To serve, thaw in the refrigerator for 12 hours. Bake at 350 °F (180 °C) for 25 minutes or until cheese is melted and the casserole is heated through.

Turkey Casserole

Ingredients

2 tbsp. of olive oil
1 tbsp. butter
4 turkey breast fillets
1 tsp salt
1/2 tsp pepper
2 onions, sliced thin
2 carrots, sliced
2 cups of chicken broth

Method

Preheat the oven to 350 ° F (180 °C). Heat the oil and butter in a skillet over medium heat until the butter has melted. Add the turkey and season with salt and pepper. Cook, turning occasionally, for 10 minutes or until lightly browned. Place the browned turkey fillets in a casserole dish and add vegetables and broth. Cover the dish and bake 40 minutes or until the vegetables are tender.
Remove from heat and allow turkey and vegetables to cool. Place into air-tight freezer containers. Freeze for up to 3 months.
To serve, thaw in refrigerator for 12 hours. Transfer to large pan and heat over stove.

Crock Pot Meals

Prepare your ingredients and store them in the freezer in ziploc baggies, so all you need to do is place the ingredients into the crock pot or slow cooker in the morning, and leave the meal to cook itself!

Times may vary but plan on cooking a frozen meal in the crockpot 8-10 hours on low, 6-8 hours on high. You can unthaw overnight in the refrigerator and then place in crockpot in the morning. I like to do this because if I take the frozen bag of food straight from the freezer to the crockpot I find it hard to fit it in my crockpot versus slightly unthawed in the morning I can place in the crockpot easier. You might not have this problem if you have a larger crockpot.

Creamy Peanut Butter Chicken

Ingredients
1/3 Cup creamy peanut butter
2 Tablespoons soy sauce
3 Tablespoons orange juice
Salt and pepper
6 chicken breasts

Method
Mix peanut butter, soy sauce, juice and spices in a jug. Place chicken breasts in a ziploc baggie and pour sauce over chicken pieces. Seal tightly and double bag for extra security. Label bag and place in freezer.
To cook, unthaw the bag in the refrigerator overnight and then pour the contents into
the crockpot the next morning. Cook on low for 6-8 hours. Serve with rice and steamed vegetables or salad.

Tropical Pork Roast

Ingredients
1/2 cup soy sauce
2 tbsp. brown sugar
8 oz. crushed pineapple
dash ground ginger
salt and pepper to taste
3 lb. (1kg) boneless pork roast

Method
Whisk soy sauce sugar, pineapple and seasonings. Place pork roast in a large ziplock bag and pour marinade over pork. Double bag and place in freezer.
To serve, thaw in refrigerator for 12 hours, then place pork and marinade in crock pot and cook on low heat for 6 to 7 hours.

Chunky Beef Casserole

Ingredients

4 tbsp. olive oil
2 onions, chopped
1 1/2 lb. (700g) diced lean beef
8 garlic cloves, minced
1 1/4 cups beef broth
2 (28 oz.) cans tomatoes, chopped
4 bay leaves
1/8 tsp thyme
1/2 tsp salt
1/2 tsp pepper

Method

Heat oil in pan and add onions. Cook until soft. Stir in the beef and stir until cooked through. Add in the garlic and stirring constantly cook for 1 minute. Add the broth and simmer for 5 minutes. Stir in the tomatoes, bay leaves, thyme, salt and pepper. Bring the mixture to a boil, reduce the heat to low and simmer 30 minutes. Let the mixture cool to room temperature. remove bay leaves. Transfer to freezer containers and freeze for up to 6 months.

To serve, thaw in refrigerator for 12 hours, then place in crock pot and cook on low heat for 6 to 7 hours.

Serve with rice or mashed potatoes, and steamed vegetables.

Slow Cooked Chicken in Barbeque Sauce

Ingredients

1 whole chicken, cut into 8 pieces and skinned
1 cup catsup
1 tablespoon brown sugar, firmly packed
3 tablespoons Worcestershire sauce

Method

Place sugar, catsup and brown sugar. In a jug and mix well. Place the chicken pieces into a Ziploc bag and pour sauce mixture over chicken. Double-bag the chicken for security, and place the bag in the freezer.
Unthaw chicken overnight and place in crock pot in the morning. Cook on low 6-8 hours.

Three Bean Pork Stew

Ingredients
6 tbsp. of oil
3 onions, chopped
6 ribs of celery, chopped small
2 lb. lean pork, cut into 1/2 in cubes
2 tsp paprika
14 oz. (40g) cannellini beans
14 oz. (40g) lima beans
14 oz. (40g) kidney beans
8 garlic cloves, minced
1 3/4 cup of vegetable broth
Juice from 1 lemon
1/2 tsp salt
1/4 tsp pepper

Method
Heat oil in pan and add onions and celery. Cook, stirring until soft. Add pork and cook 10 minutes until cooked through. Sprinkle the paprika over the top. Add beans and stir to combine. Stir in the garlic and cook the mixture 1 minute.

Pour in the broth and lemon juice, stirring to combine well. Season with salt and pepper. Bring the mixture to a boil, reduce the heat and simmer 20 minutes.

Cool completely before placing in air-tight container and freezing for up to 3 months.

To serve, thaw in the refrigerator for 12 hours. Heat in a saucepan, stirring regularly until heated through.

Chalupa Crockpot

Ingredients
1-2 lb. (500g – 1kg) Beef Roast
1-2 lb. (500g – 1kg) Pork roast
1/2 cup water
2 cups salsa
1/2 cup chopped onion
2 cups cooked pinto beans

Method
Season roasts with salt and pepper and place in crock pot. Add water and cook for several hours until cooked through. Cool and shred meats, mixing them together. Stir in salsa, chopped onions and pinto beans. Cool and freeze in air-tight container.
To serve, thaw for 12 hours in refrigerator and reheat. Serve wrapped in tortillas or with corn chips, salsa, avocado and sour cream.
Serve meat mixture wrapped in a tortilla, on corn chips or tortilla chips, add shredded cheese, salsa, avocado, olives or sour cream.

Cheesy Ham & Chicken Casserole

Ingredients

1 can (10 oz.) Cheddar cheese soup, condensed
1 can (14 oz.) diced tomatoes
1/2 cup water
1 1/2 lbs. (700 g) chicken pieces
1 cup diced cooked ham

Method

Blend soup, tomatoes and water in a jug until well combined. Place chicken pieces and ham in a ziplock bag and pour soup mixture over the top. Seal tightly and double bag.

To prepare, place in a crock pot at low heat for 7 hours. Serve with rice or mashed potato and vegetables.

Lemon Teriyaki Chicken

Ingredients

1/2 Cup lemon juice
1/2 Cup soy sauce
1/4 Cup sugar
3 Tablespoons brown sugar
2 Tablespoons water
2 garlic cloves chopped
1/2 teaspoon ginger
6 chicken breasts, sliced

Method

Combine sauces, sugars, water, garlic and ginger into a ziploc bag. Add except chicken. Blend together. Add chicken pieces and double bag. Freeze.
To prepare, place in a crock pot at low heat for 8 hours.
If you'd rather bake in the oven, thaw for 12 hours then bake in casserole dish or cook in skillet until chicken is cooked through.

Sweet and Sour Chicken
Ingredients
4 chicken breasts, cubed
can pineapple chunks, drained
1 garlic clove, minced
2-3 Tablespoons soy sauce
l teaspoon ginger
1-2 carrots cut in small pieces
1 green, yellow or red pepper cut in pieces

Method
Combine all ingredients in a ziploc bag. Shake until
chicken is well coated. Double-bag and freeze.

To serve, thaw in refrigerator for 12 hours. To prepare,
place in a crock pot at low heat for 8 hours.
Serve with rice and steamed vegetables.

Marinated Teriyaki Beef

Ingredients
1/2 cup orange juice
1/4 cup soy sauce
2 tbsp. onion powder
2 tbsp. brown sugar
1 garlic clove minced
1/4 teaspoon ginger
1 lb. (500g) cubed beef

Method
Mix marinade ingredients together in a jug. Place beef in a ziplock bag and pour marinade into the bag, coating beef thoroughly. Double-bag and freeze.
To serve, thaw for 12 hours in refrigerator, to prepare, place in a crock pot at low heat for 8 hours.

Chicken Salsa

Ingredients

4 chicken breasts
1 jar salsa
1 can black beans (drained)
1 can corn (drained)

Method

Place all ingredients in a ziplock bag and freeze. To prepare, place frozen contents into a crock pot and cook on low for 6-8 hours.

Minestrone Soup
Ingredients
Chopped sausage
1 onion, diced
1 cup carrot, diced
1 small zucchini, diced
1/2 cup chopped celery
4 cups chicken stock
1 lb. (500g) kidney beans
2 lb. (1 kg) crushed tomatoes
2 tablespoons basil
2 tablespoons oregano
Parmesan cheese

Method
Cook sausage and onion together in a pan. Drain and let cool. In a ziploc bag or container, Add sausage, onion and remaining ingredients. Freeze. To serve, thaw for 12 hours in refrigerator, to prepare, place in a crock pot at low heat and cook for 6-7 hours. 30 minutes before serving, add 1/2 Cup pasta.

Chicken Vegetable Chili Soup

Ingredients

1 lb. (500g) ground chicken
1 onion, grated
2 lb. (1kg) diced tomatoes
1/2 cup tomato sauce
1 tablespoon chili powder
1 teaspoon cumin
1/2 teaspoon salt
3 cups chili beans or black beans soaked overnight and cooked

Method

In large pan cook hamburger and grated onion until hamburger is browned. Drain and let cool. Add mixture to ziploc bag or container. Add diced tomatoes, tomato sauce, chili powder, cumin, seasoning salt and beans. Freeze.
To prepare, place in a crock pot at low heat and cook for 6-7 hours.

Tomato Chili Soup

Ingredients

1 lb. (500g) ground beef steak
1 l onion, diced finely
2 garlic cloves, minced
2 lb. (1kg) tomatoes, diced and pureed
15 oz. (2 cups) tomato sauce
1 tablespoon chili powder
1 t ground cumin
1/2 teaspoon salt
1/4 teaspoon pepper
2 lb. (900g) chili beans
1/4 cup water, optional

Method

Cook the onion in a large skillet over medium heat and add the beef and garlic. Cook stirring, until beef is brown and onion is soft. Drain fat from meat. Set aside.
Combine tomatoes, tomato sauce, chili powder and cumin into a ziploc bag or freezer container. Season with salt and pepper. Add the meat and beans. Seal and freeze.

To prepare, place in a crock pot at low heat and cook for 7-8 hours.

Tomato Onion Soup

Ingredients

3 tbsp. canola oil
3 onions, chopped very fine
4 garlic cloves, minced
30 tomatoes, quartered
1/2 tsp salt
1/4 tsp pepper
2 tsp sugar
1 tbsp. tomato paste
2 1/2 cups of vegetable stock

Method

Place the oil a pan and cook the onions, stirring until soft.
Add the garlic and tomatoes and season to taste with the salt
and pepper. Add the sugar and tomato paste and stir until
blended in well. Cook over very low heat, stirring often, for
30 minutes.
Adjust the heat to medium high and add the stock. Bring the
mixture to a rapid boil then reduce the heat back to low.
Cook the soup for 10 minutes. Place the soup in batches,
into a food processor and puree until smooth. Cool the soup
at room temperature, then pour into freezer containers and
freeze for up to 3 months.

To prepare, place in a crock pot at low heat and cook for 6-7
hours.

Citrus Beef Soup

Ingredients

3 tbsp. extra virgin olive oil
3 lbs. (1.3kg) beef stew meat
1/2 tsp salt
1/4 tsp pepper
7 1/2 Cups beef or vegetable broth
3 bay leaves
2 cinnamon sticks
1.75lb (800g) chickpeas
2 oranges, peeled and sectioned

Method

Pour the oil into a large skillet. Season the beef with the salt and pepper and place into the skillet. Stir the beef over medium heat for 10 minutes, until browned. in a freezer container or bag, pour the broth, meat mixture, bay leaves, cinnamon stick and chickpeas. Add orange sections and store in freezer containers.

Freeze for up to 3 months in the freezer. To thaw, place container in refrigerator for 12 hours., To prepare, place in a crock pot at low heat and cook for 7-8 hours.

Thick Beef Soup

Ingredients

1-2 lbs. (500g-1kg) beef stew meat
In a skillet, cook meat in a small amount of oil.
Meanwhile in a large measuring cup or bowl stir together:
2 Cups beef broth
1 teaspoon Worcestershire sauce
1 clove garlic
1/2 teaspoon Paprika
2 teaspoon salt
2 teaspoons brown sugar
3 carrots, sliced
3 potatoes, diced
1 onion, chopped
1 stalk celery, chopped

Method

Cook stew meat in a skillet until brown. Set aside to cool.
Combine broth, Worcestershire sauce, garlic, paprika, salt
and pepper in a freezer container. Allow meat to cool and
place in container. Add chopped vegetables to the bag. Seal
and freeze.
Thaw for 12 hours in refrigerator, then cook on high in
crock pot for 8 hours.

Condiments

Freezing home-made condiments is both cost-effective and practical. Condiments are best made in bulk, but even a large family would struggle to consume buckets of home-made jam and tomato sauce. When you freeze the produce in small portions, it is always fresh and always available at a fraction of the price of store-bought condiments.

Here are some tips for how you can save time and money by freezing your own home-made condiments.

Instant apple pie filling: During apple season, slice and flash freeze a bulk load of apples, then freeze in filling-size batches. All year round, you will have instant fresh apples when you want to make pie.

Ready-cut onion: Always have chopped or sliced onion on hand, by cutting a bulk amount and freezing them in a container. Store chopped onion separately from sliced onion and take out a handful whenever required for cooking.

Store your salsa: Harvest your own tomatoes or bulk-buy them while in season and make salsa to be used as a dipping sauce or tasty ingredient. Store it in small plastic containers so you only ever thaw the amount you can use immediately.

Stock up on jam: Make your favorite jams and chutneys using seasonal fruits and berries and freeze them in small containers so you only thaw as much as you need.

Make your own BBQ sauce: For genuine delicious flavor, make your own tomato sauce or barbecue sauce and freeze in small portions. BBQ also works as an easy marinade if you freeze it with chicken breasts.

Apple sauce: Quick and easy to make, apple sauce is a great standby in the freezer as you can serve it with pork or throw it into muffins or cakes for some extra fruit flavor.

Homemade pesto: The perfect accompaniment to pasta, you can make pesto with home-grown or bulk-buy basil.

Ice cube tips and tricks

Your ice cube trays can do more than simply store ice for a party – you can also keep some fresh and savory ingredients on hand, whether you need to give your cooking an extra kick.

Herb butter cubes: Blend butter with garlic or herbs and freeze in an ice cube tray. Now each frozen butter cube gives you exactly the right amount of butter to make garlic bread, flavor a roast or a sauce, or melt over steaks.

Instant fresh herbs: Place fresh chopped herbs into an ice cube tray and cover with boiling water, then freeze. Once the cubes are frozen, you can remove them from your ice cube tray and store the cubes in a zip lock bag. The cubes are ready whenever you need some extra herbs for soups or sauces. You can also store minced garlic in the same way, so long as you use oil rather than water in the cubes.

Instant eggs:

Freeze eggs by breaking each egg into a separate compartment of an ice cube tray. When you need an egg for cooking, pop one from the tray and leave it to thaw in the refrigerator.

Classic Strawberry Freezer Jam

Ingredients

2 cups strawberries, washed and hulled
7 cups sugar
2 pkgs (1 3/4 oz.) powdered pectin
1 cup cold water
4 1-pt (500ml) lidded freezer containers

Method

Wash and hull strawberries and mash with a fork. Stir in sugar until strawberries are well coated. Set aside.

Place cold water and pectin in pan. Bring to a boil over medium heat, stirring constantly. Boil for 1 minute before removing from heat. Add mixture to mashed fruit and stir for about 4 minutes to combine.

Pour into storage containers. Allow to sit for 12 hours, then place in freezer.

Pine-Berry Freezer Jam

Ingredients

2 1/2 cups fresh strawberries, washed and hulled
2 1/2 cups fresh pineapple, peeled and finely chopped
7 cups sugar
2 pkgs (1 3/4 oz.) powdered pectin
1 cup cold water
4 1-pt (500ml) lidded freezer containers

Method

Place strawberries in a large mixing bowl and mash with a fork. Add the pineapple and then stir in sugar slowly until well combined.

Place the cold water and pectin in a pan over medium heat, stirring continuously until water begins to boil. Boil 1 minute.

Remove from heat. Pour pectin mixture over the fruit and stir well to combine.

Continue stirring 4 minutes. Pour into the freezer containers and cover. Allow to sit at room temperature for 24 hours then freeze for up to 6 months. To use, remove from freezer and thaw at room temperature for about 1 hour. Cover and refrigerate for up to 3 weeks.

Peach Freezer Jam

Ingredients

3 lbs. peaches, peeled and pitted
5 cups sugar
2 pkgs (1 3/4 oz.) powdered pectin
1 cup cold water
4 1-pt (500ml) lidded freezer containers

Method

Chop or mash peaches and stir in sugar until well combined. Place the cold water and pectin in a pan over medium heat, stirring continuously until water begins to boil. Boil 1 minute.

Remove from heat. Pour pectin mixture over the fruit and stir well to combine.

Continue stirring 4 minutes. Pour into the freezer containers and cover. Allow to sit at room temperature for 24 hours then freeze for up to 6 months. To use, remove from freezer and thaw at room temperature for about 1 hour. Cover and refrigerate for up to 3 weeks.

Ginger Peach Freezer Jam

Ingredients

4 cups peaches, peeled, pitted and chopped finely
2 tablespoon ginger
5 cups sugar
2 pkgs (1 3/4 oz.) powdered pectin
1 cup cold water
4 (1 pint) freezer containers with lids

Method

Place peaches in a large mixing bowl and add ginger. Stir together while slowly adding the sugar. Mix until well combined.

Place the cold water in a small saucepan and place over medium heat. Add the pectin. Bring to a boil, stirring continuously. Boil for 1 minute.

Remove from heat and pour over fruit. Stir until all is combined. Continue to stir 4 minutes. Pour mixture into containers and cover with lids. Leave standing at room temperature for 24 hours.

Freeze for up to 6 months. When ready to use remove from freezer and allow coming to room temperature about 1 to 2 hours. Freezer jam will stay good in the refrigerator for up to 3 weeks.

Classic Barbecue Sauce

Ingredients

1 cup water
4 tablespoons sugar
2 teaspoon salt
1/2 cup red wine vinegar
2 tablespoon mustard
1 teaspoon pepper
1 cup ketchup or tomato paste
4 tablespoons Worcestershire sauce
3 1-cup capacity freezer containers

Method

Blend all ingredients in a bowl until well combined. Divide between freezer containers and freeze.

Classic Hummus Dip

Ingredients

15 oz. can of garbanzo beans
1 garlic clove, chopped
1 teaspoon salt
1/4 cup cold water
5 tablespoons lemon juice
1/3 cup tahini paste (if you can't locate tahini paste, use sesame seeds)

Method

Blend all ingredients until smooth and freeze in small containers. To serve, thaw at room temperature for 12 hours.

Teriyaki Sauce

Ingredients
1/2 cup soy sauce
2 tablespoons Worcestershire sauce
1/2 cup brown sugar
1/2 cup water
4 teaspoon ginger
2 garlic clove minced

Method
Blend ingredients until well combined. Store in small freezer containers and thaw at room temperature if required as a dipping sauce. Alternately, to make a teriyaki chicken freezer meal, pour over chicken pieces in a Ziploc bag and freeze. To serve, thaw in refrigerator for 12 hours and stir fry to cook.

Cucumber Pickles

Ingredients

6 cucumbers, thinly sliced
1 red onion, thinly sliced
2 tablespoon salt
1 cup white vinegar
3/4 cup sugar
Freezer containers

Method

Combine cucumbers and onions in a large mixing bowl and add salt. Let stand at room temperature for 2 hours then rinse in cool water and drain well. Mix the vinegar and sugar until the sugar is completely dissolved. Place the cucumber and onion blend into freezer containers and pour the vinegar mixture over the top. Seal container and freeze for at least 3 weeks before serving.
Thaw in the refrigerator for 12 hours.

Breads and Baking

Home-made bread is a great addition to any meal, whether it is a crusty loaf with cold meat and homemade condiments for lunch, dinner rolls with your main meal, or even a bread bowl for serving soup or dip.

To keep a supply of bread in your freezer, you can either freeze baked bread or dough which has already had one rising.

Tips for Using Bread Dough

Freeze your bread dough into small dinner-roll portions so you only thaw out as much as you need. Some of these ideas require a few balls of dough.

Ready-bake dinner rolls or breadsticks

Shape the dough into small rolls before freezing so they are ready to bake when you want to serve bread with dinner. Alternately, combine two balls of dough and roll into a bread stick. Sprinkle with garlic salt and cheese before baking for a savory finish.

Stromboli

Thaw out about 4 balls of dough and roll into a rectangle. Top with tomato paste, diced ham or bacon and cheese (or other pizza toppings of your choice). Roll up the rectangle into a jelly roll shape, and bake until bread is cooked through.

Sweet or savory bubble bread (or monkey bread)

Divide balls into smaller balls. For sweet bubble bread, combine equal quantities of sugar and cinnamon and roll the small balls in the mixture until well coated. For savory bubble bread, roll the balls in seasoned parmesan cheese.

Place the balls together in the shape of a loaf or cake, as desired, and bake until bread is cooked through.

Tacos
Roll balls flat and fry the dough to make tacos.

Basic Breads

Basic Freezer Bread Dough

This recipe makes 4 loaves of bread and is ideal for freezing.

Ingredients

2 tablespoons yeast
1 pinch sugar
1/2 cup warm water
4 cups warm water
1/2 cup oil
2 tablespoon salt
2/3 cup brown sugar
6 cups whole wheat flour
2 cups white flour

Method

Mix yeast with 1/2 cup warm water in a jug and add sugar. Set aside.

Combine 4 cups warm water, oil, salt and brown sugar. Add yeast.

Add 4-5 Cups whole wheat flour to mixture and blend together until well combined. Add remaining flour one cup at a time. Knead dough for several minutes.

Place 1 tablespoon oil in the base of a large bowl and add bread dough. Cover and leave to rise until it doubles.

Separate into 4 portions and freeze in air-tight freezer bags. When ready to use, remove from freezer and allow to thaw at room temperature for 12 hours. Once the dough reaches room temperature, allow it to rise again, then shape as desired. Bake at 350 ° F (180 ºC) until golden brown.

Stuffed hamburger rolls

Ingredients

Frozen rolls of bread dough
1 lb. (550g) ground hamburger
salt and pepper
1 onion, sliced
1/2 cup shredded cabbage
3 tbsp. tomato paste

Method

Heat oil in pan and add onion. Cook until soft then add hamburger meat and cook until brown. Add tomato paste and stir through. Drain fat, then add cabbage and season to taste.

Roll each ball flat and cut into small circles. Place a tablespoon of beef mixture onto each circle and fold over, pressing edges together to seal. Bake at 350 ° F (180 ºC) for 10-15 minutes or until golden brown.

Clover Leaf Rolls

Ingredients

1 3/4 cup warm water
2 pkg active dry yeast
1/2 cup sugar
1 tablespoon salt
1 egg
1/4 cup soft butter or margarine
6 cups sifted all purpose (plain) flour
1 tablespoon butter or margarine, melted
Freezer paper

Method

Rinse a large bowl with hot water. Pour the warm water into the bowl and add the yeast, sugar and salt. Stir until completely dissolved.

Add the egg, soft butter and 3 cups of flour, beating with an electric mixer on medium speed until smooth. Slowly add 1 more cup of flour and continue beating for 2 minutes.

Add the remaining 2 cups of flour to the mixture and work the flour, using your hands. Continue until all the flour is well combined and the mixture becomes smooth and elastic.

Shape the dough into a ball and brush the top with melted butter. Cover the bowl with a damp towel and place in the refrigerator to rise for 2 hours or until double in size.

Punch down the dough then keep dough covered and stored in refrigerator for 1-3 days until ready for baking. If you are storing for more than one day, punch the dough once a day until ready for use.

Preheat oven to 375°F (190°C). To make the rolls, divide the dough into 3 equal portions. Take one portion and divide it into half. Roll each half into a 16 inch (40cm) long rope. Cut each rope into 18 pieces. Roll each piece into a smooth ball.

Line a muffin pan with paper cups. Place three balls in each cup, overlapping to make a clover shape. Cover the muffin trays with a towel and place in a warm position to rise for 1 hour or until dough has doubled in size. Bake rolls for 20 minutes. Remove and cool completely.

Wrap rolls in freezer paper and freeze for up to 12 months. To serve, preheat oven to 450 ºF (230 ºC) and place unwrapped rolls on cookie sheet. Bake 5 to 10 minutes or until light brown.

Freezer Pie Crust

Ingredients
2 cups sifted all purpose (plain) flour
1 teaspoon salt
3/4 cup shortening
4 to 5 tablespoons ice water
Wax paper
Freezer wrap

Method
Combine flour and salt in a large mixing bowl. Using a pastry blender, cut in the shortening until mixture become crumbly. Add 1 tablespoon of the ice water at a time, tossing with a fork after each addition. Continue adding ice water until all dry ingredients are evenly moistened, but do not allow the mixture to become sticky.
Divide dough in half and roll each half into a ball.
Wrap each ball with wax paper and then wrap tightly in the freezer wrap. Freeze for up to 2 months.
To use, thaw at room temperature and roll out as desired.
~ If you'd prefer you can roll dough out flat and place in tin foil pie plates. Wrap and freeze. This makes it even easier to pull out a readymade pie crust.

Freezer Pizza Crust

Ingredients
2 1/4 cups water
3 tbsp. extra virgin olive oil
2 tsp salt
2 tbsp. sugar
2 cups of whole wheat flour
3 3/4 cups of bread flour
2 tsp instant yeast

Method
Place all ingredients into the baking pan of the bread machine and set to dough cycle. Once the dough has been mixed, remove it from the machine and place on a lightly floured flat surface. Cover the dough and let it rest for 10 minutes. Preheat oven to 400 °F (205 °C).
Divide the dough into three portions, and press each portion onto a lightly greased 12" or 14" pizza pan, or make individual size pizza crusts. Partially bake the crusts for 10 minutes. After cooking allow the crusts to cool at room temperature, then freeze in an airtight container for up to 2 months.
To prepare, remove from freezer and add your topping of choice and cheese. Bake at 400 °F (205 °C) for 20 minutes until the pizza is hot and the cheese has melted.

Home-made Freezer Pasta

Ingredients

2/3 cup water

1 egg

2 tbsp. extra chili-infused virgin olive oil

1 tsp salt

2 1/2 cups semolina flour

Method

Place all ingredients into the bread pan of your bread machine your bread machine and set to the pasta or dough cycle. When the cycle is complete, remove the dough to a lightly floured flat surface and divide the dough into 5 portions. Place each portion into a plastic bag to keep them from drying out.

Working with one portion at a time, roll and fold the dough repeatedly, until you achieve a smooth elastic texture. If the dough is sticky, dust with flour; if it is too dry add a teaspoon of water.

Once the dough is smooth, roll it out until it is 1/8 inch to 1/4 inch thick. Cut the dough as desired for your recipe. Place the dough into a large pot of salted boiling water and boil for 5 minutes or until the pasta reached the desired consistency.

Rinse cooked pasta under cold water and store in the freezer for up to 1 month.

Fruit or Vegetable Breads

Choc-Chip Banana Loaf (or muffins)

Ingredients

3/4 cup white sugar
3/4 cup brown sugar
3/4 cup butter or margarine
4 eggs
1 teaspoon vanilla
4 mashed bananas
1/2 teaspoon soda
2 Cups white flour
1 1/2 cups wheat flour
1 teaspoon salt
1 cup chocolate chips

Method

Mash bananas with baking soda and set aside.
Combine sugars, butter, eggs, vanilla and salt.
Blend in flours and banana mixture in mixing bowl. Blend until well combined. Add chocolate chips and stir until well combined. Pour batter in greased loaf pan or muffin pans and bake 350 ° F (180 °C) 45-50 minutes if cooking a loaf or 15-20 minutes for muffin cups, until cooked through and golden brown.
Allow to cool and freeze in air-tight freezer bags.

Pineapple Carrot Loaf (or muffins)

Ingredients

1 teaspoon ginger
3 eggs
1 cup vegetable oil
1 1/2 cups sugar
2 cups carrots, shredded
8-ounce (225g) crushed pineapple
1 1/2 cup white flour
1 1/2 cup wheat flour
1/2 teaspoon baking powder
1 teaspoon baking soda
1 teaspoon salt

Method

Blend eggs, oil, sugar, ginger, carrots and pineapple in a bowl. Add flours, baking powder, baking soda and salt and stir until well combined. Pour into greased loaf pans or muffin cups. Bake at 350 ° F (180 ºC) about 45-50 minutes if cooking a loaf or 15-20 minutes for muffin cups.

Zucchini Bread or Muffins

Ingredients

2 cups grated or pureed zucchini
3 eggs
2 cups sugar
1 cup oil
3 teaspoons Vanilla
2 cups white flour
1 1/2 cups wheat flour
1 teaspoon baking soda
1/4 teaspoon baking powder
1 teaspoon salt
3 teaspoon cinnamon

Method

Combine grated zucchini, eggs, sugar, oil and vanilla in a bowl and blend well. Add flours, baking soda, baking powder, salt and cinnamon. Mix together. Cook in greased bread loaves, mini loaves or muffins. Bake 350 ° F (180 °C) until toothpick inserted comes out clean. Allow to cool and freeze in freezer bags.

Soups

Soups are ideal for freezing, as they are easy to make in bulk, they have a high water content so they thaw well and they are easy to reheat and serve, with perhaps just some bread for accompaniment.

Lentil Soup

Ingredients

2 tablespoons olive oil
1 onion chopped
3 carrots grated
3/4 teaspoon marjoram
2 lb. (1kg) tomatoes
7 cups beef or chicken stock
1 1/2 cups dried lentils

Method

Heat oil in pan and sauté onions and carrots until tender.
Puree tomatoes in a blender and add to saucepan. Add broth, onion mixture and lentils. Cook on medium-low in a covered pan for one hour or until lentils are tender. Season to taste.
Allow to cool and pour into freezer containers.
When reheating, add cooked pasta and stir through.

Ham and Bean Soup

Ingredients

2 cups dried beans
8 cups water
1 onion, chopped
1 teaspoon chili powder
1 ham bone
1 garlic clove
2 lb. (1kg) tomatoes, pureed
1 bay leaf
1/2 teaspoon salt
1/4 teaspoon pepper
2 tablespoons lemon juice

Method

Soak beans overnight. Cover beans with water in a large pot and bring to a boil. Remove from heat, cover and let stand 1 hour. Drain water and rinse. Add remaining ingredients and simmer for an additional hour and 15 minutes.
Allow to cool and place into freezer containers.

Beef & Barley Soup

Ingredients

1 lb. (500g) ground beef
1 onion chopped
2 teaspoons oregano
2 lb. (1kg) tomatoes, pureed
4 cups beef broth or stock
2/3 cup barley, uncooked

Method

Heat oil in pan and cook onion until soft. Add beef and cook until brown. Season to taste and drain fat from meat. In a soup pan, combine meat with pureed tomatoes, barley, and beef broth. Cook until barley is tender. Allow to cool and pour in freezer containers.

Classic Chicken Broth

Ingredients

14 cups water
4 lb. (2kg) whole chickens
2 large carrots
2 onions, quartered
6 cloves garlic, peeled
2 bay leaves
2 celery stalks including celery leaves
2 teaspoons salt
1 tablespoon parsley

Method

Place all ingredients in a large pot and bring to a boil. Reduce
heat to medium-low and allow to simmer for 1 hour. Allow to
cool slightly and strain broth into a pan to cool completely.
Once chicken is cool enough to handle, shred meat from the
bone. (You can use this chicken meat for other recipes). Strain
vegetables from broth, and freeze broth to use as a base for
soup or eat as a soup as it is, with some added vegetables and/
or pasta.

Cream of potato soup
Ingredients
2 cups potatoes, cubed
1 small onion, diced
1 carrot
1 celery stalk
1 cup cauliflower pieces
Water
2 teaspoons chicken bouillon
1/4 Cup milk

Method
Cut vegetables into slices or cubes. Place potatoes, onion, carrot, celery and cauliflower in a large pan. Add sufficient water to cover vegetables. Cook and simmer on medium until vegetables are tender. Add half of soup mixture into blender. Add bouillon and milk to blender and puree several seconds. Return to saucepan and stir to combine. Allow to cool and freeze in smaller containers.

Chunky Vegetable Soup

Ingredients

2 tbsp. olive oil
2 onions, finely chopped
4 garlic cloves, minced
4 celery ribs, finely chopped
4 carrots, chopped
1 tsp rosemary
4 small zucchini, cut into cubes
2 lb. (1kg) whole tomatoes, chopped
4 cups of vegetable stock
1/2 tsp salt
1/4 tsp pepper

Method

Place the oil into a large saucepan and cook the onions, stirring often, until soft.

Add the garlic, celery, carrots and rosemary. Cook the mixture, stirring occasionally, for 10 minutes before adding the zucchini and cook for a further 5 minutes. Stir in the tomatoes, then pour in the stock. Season to taste while stirring constantly.

Bring the mixture to a rapid boil then reduce the heat to low and simmer for 20 minutes. Allow to cool to room temperature. Transfer to freezer containers and freeze for up to 3 months. To reheat, thaw completely in the refrigerator then heat in a saucepan on low until completely heated through.

Creamy Cauliflower Soup

Ingredients

2 tbsp. of olive oil
2 onions, chopped
3 garlic cloves, minced
4 celery ribs, chopped fine
2 bay leaves
1 1/2 lbs. potatoes cut in cubes
1/2 tsp salt
1/2 tsp pepper
15 C of vegetable broth
2 heads of cauliflower, trimmed and cut into florets

Method

Heat the oil in a large soup pan over low heat. Add the onions and cook until just soft.
Stir in the garlic, celery and bay leaf and cook until the celery is soft. Add the potatoes and season with salt and pepper. Cook the mixture, stirring well, for 5 minutes. Add the broth and raise the heat to medium high. Bring to a boil, then continue cooking for 15 minutes until the potatoes start to soften. Add cauliflower and cook 15 minutes, stirring until the cauliflower has softened. Remove the bay leaves and pour the soup into the blender or food processor. Blend until smooth.
Cool the soup at room temperature then transfer to freezer containers.
This soup will stay fresh in the freezer for up to 2 months. To reheat, thaw completely in the refrigerator. Place in a saucepan over low heat and stirring often, cook until heated through. Once heated, stir through sufficient heavy cream to achieve desired thickness.

Pizza Soup

Ingredients

8 oz. (225g) sliced mushrooms
8 oz. (225g) black olives sliced
4 cups water
15 oz. (425g) tomato paste
2 tablespoons Italian seasoning
chopped pepperoni
chopped green peppers

Method

Combine all ingredients and simmer 15-20 minutes. Cool before freezing. To thaw, run container under hot water, and place frozen soup into pan. Heat over medium high until heated through.

Beef & Bean Soup

Ingredients

2 lb. (1kg) kidney beans
2 lb. (1kg) tomatoes
2 lb. (1kg) ground beef
1 cup water
2-3 Tablespoons taco seasoning

Method

Brown meat, then combine all ingredients together in saucepan. Bring to the boil then simmer for 15 minutes. Cool before freezing. Add a dollop of sour cream before serving, and serve with tortilla chips.

Chunky Garlic Seafood Soup

Ingredients

1/2 cup olive oil
1 clove garlic, chopped fine
1 medium onion, chopped
2 green onions, chopped
1 green pepper, chopped
15 oz. (425g) diced tomatoes
3 tablespoons tomato paste
1 3/4 cup burgundy
1 tablespoon parsley
2 teaspoon oregano
1/2 teaspoon basil
2 teaspoon salt
1/4 teaspoon pepper
3/4 cup water
1 1/2 lb. (700g) halibut steaks, chopped into chunks
1/2 raw shrimp, shelled and de-veined
2 (6 oz./170g) pkgs frozen crabmeat, thawed

Method

Heat oil in a large pan over medium heat. Add the garlic, onion, green onion and
green pepper. Cook until tender. Add the tomatoes and the tomato paste then slowly add the burgundy, stirring well after each addition. Mix in the parsley, oregano, basil salt and pepper until well combined.

Add the water and bring to a rapid boil. Reduce heat to low. Simmer uncovered 1- minutes. Add seafood. Cover and simmer 15 minutes. Remove lid and cook for another
15 minutes. Remove from heat and cool to room temperature. To freeze, line a large container with foil, allowing the foil to generously overlap the edges of the container. Pour the stew into the container and fold the foil over the top of the container and secure ends firmly. Cover with more foil if necessary.

Freeze until firm, then wrap entire package with another layer of foil. Freeze for up to 6 months.
To cook, remove foil. Place frozen block in a large pan. Add 1 cup water. Cover and cook on low until heated through.

Desserts

It's always helpful to have a delicious dessert on hand for unexpected guests. These desserts are easy to prepare in advance and freeze beautifully.

Freezing Cookie Dough

Prepare your favorite cookie dough and roll into logs.
Wrap up in plastic wrap and tin foil and freeze.
Dough freezes well and only needs to unthaw about 30 minutes
-1 hour.
Slice the log and bake.

Choc-Mint Angel Cake

Ingredients
1 (15 oz.) pkg Angel Food Cake Mix
1/3 cup chocolate mint cookies, crushed
3/4 cup chopped pecans (optional)
6 cups peppermint ice cream, slightly soft
Aluminum foil
Freezer wrap

Method
Preheat oven to 375°F (190°C). Mix cake batter as directed
on the package. Pour the batter into an un-greased 10-in
tube pan. Bake cake on the lowest oven shelf for 35 minutes.
Remove cake from pan and allow to cool for about 1 hour.
Place the ice cream into a large mixing bowl with cookies
and pecans and combine well.
Place the ice cream mixture back in the freezer for about 5
minutes.
Cut the cake into three sections lengthwise. Place one
section of
the cake on a sheet of aluminum foil large enough to wrap
the entire cake when completed. Remove ice cream and
spread 1/3 of the mixture over the top of the cake. Add
another section of cake. Spread another 1/3 of the ice cream
mixture. Place the last section of cake on top. Finish with
the rest of the ice cream. Cover tightly with the aluminum
foil. Place in freezer for 2 hours.
Remove from freezer and wrap in the freezer wrap. Cake
can be stored in the freezer for up to 1 month.
To serve, remove from freezer. Unwrap and allow to set for
about 10 minutes. Slice and serve.

Plum Pie Filling

Ingredients

2 tablespoons lemon juice
4 cups purple plums, sliced
1 cups sugar
2 tablespoons quick cooking tapioca
1/2 teaspoon cinnamon
1/2 teaspoon nutmeg
Heavy duty aluminum foil

Method

Place the plums in a large mixing bowl and sprinkle with the lemon juice.

In another bowl combine the sugar, tapioca, cinnamon and nutmeg. Add plums to the sugar mixture. Toss to cover plums completely in sugar mixture. Set aside for 15 minutes.

Place the aluminum foil in a pie plate ensuring the foil extends generously over the plate. Fill the foil with the plum filling. Fold the foil over the top.

Freeze for several hours. Wrap filling in extra foil to ensure it is secure. Freeze for up to 6 months.

To make into pie, preheat oven to 425 °F (220 °C). Thaw filling in refrigerator, and then pour into prepared pie crust. Top with another layer of pie crust and pinch the edges to seal. Slit the crust in 4 places to release steam. Bake for 45 minutes or until top is a golden brown.

Lemon Curd Cake

Ingredients

5 tbsp. of softened butter
1 cup sugar
Zest from 2 lemons and 1 orange, grated fine
3 large eggs, separated
3/4 cups of flour
1 cup of milk
Juice from 2 lemons
2 tbsp. lemon curd

Method

Preheat oven to 350 ° F (180 °C). Cream butter and sugar together, then add zest and egg yolks. Beat until well combined. Add 1/4 cup of flour and mix well to combine, then stir in 1/2 cup of milk and mix well. Repeat alternating flour and milk, ending with a flour addition. Fold in the lemon juice.

Beat the egg whites until soft peaks form. Fold the egg white mixture into the batter. Spread the lemon curd over the base of an ovenproof, freezer safe dish. Pour the batter over the curd. Place the dish in a pan filled halfway with warm water. Bake 25 minutes or until golden brown. Cool, wrap and freeze.

To serve, thaw overnight in the refrigerator. Heat the cake in a preheated 350 ° F (180 °C) oven for 25 minutes or until warmed through.

Baked Marmalade Pudding
Ingredients
4 thick slices of bread
2 tbsp. of butter at room temperature
4 tbsp. orange marmalade
1 egg
1 1/4 cup milk
2 tbsp. of sugar
1 tsp ginger

Method
Butter each slice of bread and then spread with marmalade.
Cut each slice into 4 triangles and line the base of a lightly
greased disposable baking dish.
Lightly beat the eggs, and add the milk, beating until well
combined. Mix in the sugar and ginger. Pour the mixture
over the bread and stand for 30 minutes. Bake the pudding at
350 ° F (180 °C) for 35 minutes or until set.
Cool at room temperature before freezing. Wrap baking dish
completely in foil and freeze. To reheat, thaw in refrigerator
for 12 hours and place in a preheated 350 ° F (180 °C) oven
for 30 minutes.

Devilish Mocha Pie

Ingredients
2/3 cup butter flavored syrup
2 1/2 cup toasted rice cereal
2 cups chocolate ice cream, softened
2 cups mocha flavored ice cream, softened
1/3 cup chopped pecans

Method
Place syrup in a small pan and bring to a boil. Reduce heat to low and simmer
2 minutes stirring often.
Place the cereal in a large bowl and pour the syrup over the cereal. Mix together until cereal is well coated.
Lightly butter a 9 in pie plate. Press cereal mixture evenly along the base and sides of the pie plate. Freeze 30 minutes.
Once cereal crust has set, spread the chocolate ice cream over the cereal crust and return pan to freezer until the ice cream has set firmly.
Stir the pecans through the mocha ice cream, and spread over the chocolate layer. Return to the freezer to set until firm. Once it is set, wrap the container tightly in foil and store in freezer.

Chocolate Cherry Bars
Ingredients
6 oz. (170g) butter, cut into pieces
9 oz. (255g) semisweet chocolate, broken into pieces
2 tbsp. light corn syrup
1 lb. (500g) sweet biscuits, crushed
2 tbsp. cherries, chopped
1 tbsp. pecans, chopped

Method
Lightly grease 8-inch square pan.
Place the butter, chocolate and syrup into a large saucepan over low heat and cook, stirring constantly until the chocolate is melted and all ingredients are well combined. Remove the pan from heat. Stir in the biscuits, cherries and pecans. Press the mixture into the buttered pan. Refrigerate until cooled and set. Cut into pieces, wrap and freeze. Thaw at room temperature before serving.

Mini Lemon Tarts

Ingredients

1 cup toasted rice cereal, crushed
3 eggs, separated
1/2 cup sugar
1 tablespoon lemon peel, grated
1/3 cup lemon juice
1 cup heavy whipping cream
6 small foil pie pans

Method

Beat egg whites until frothy with stiff peaks. Slowly add 2 tablespoons of sugar at a time, beating well after each addition.

In a separate bowl, beat egg yolks on medium speed until they begin to thicken. Add the lemon peel and lemon juice and mix to combine. Fold the yolk mixture into the white mixture using a rubber spatula. Add the whipping cream and fold to combine.

Press crushed cereal into the base of each of the pie pans. Fill each pie pan
with the lemon mixture. Top with more crushed cereal. Wrap tightly with the freezer paper and freeze for up to 3 months. Thaw in refrigerator for 1 hour before serving.

Ready-Made Apricot Pie Filling

Ingredients
1 tablespoon lemon juice
4 cups apricots, sliced
3/4 cup light brown sugar, packed
1/4 cup sugar
2 tablespoon quick cooking tapioca
1/2 teaspoon salt
2 T butter or margarine
Heavy duty aluminum foil

Method
In a large mixing bowl, toss apricots in lemon juice.
In a separate bowl combine brown sugar, regular sugar, tapioca and salt. Fold in the apricots so they are all well coated with the mixture. Let stand 15 minutes. Line a 9 in pie plate with the aluminum foil with generous overlap. Fill the foil with the pie filling and fold the foil over the top of the filling so it is well wrapped. Leave in freezer several hours until set, then remove from freezer and wrap in another layer of aluminum foil. Freeze for up to 6 months. To serve, remove filling from freezer and place in a prepared pie crust base. Cover filling with pie crust and crimp down the edges. Bake in a preheated oven at 425 °F (220 °C).

Peach Meringue Roll

Ingredients

4 large egg whites
Pinch of salt
1 cup + 2 tbsp. sugar
1 cup of sliced almonds
1 1/4 cup whipping cream
1 (12 oz./ 340g) can of peach halves, chopped

Method

Preheat oven to 375°F (190°C).
Beat egg whites with salt on high until stiff peaks form. Add one tablespoon of sugar at a time, while still beating. Spread the egg white evenly over the base of a lined jelly-roll pan. Spread the almonds in an even layer over the egg whites. Bake 15 minutes.
Place a sheet of parchment paper on a flat surface and dust it lightly with confectioners' sugar. Invert the warm meringue onto the parchment paper and leave it to cool.
Beat the whipping cream until stiff peaks form. Spread the beaten cream over the cooled meringue. Scatter the peaches evenly over the cream.
Starting with the short side, roll the meringue over the filling. Wrap in parchment paper and foil and freeze.
To serve, thaw in the refrigerator for 12 hours and dust with confectioners' sugar before slicing.

Apple-Berry Cobbler

Ingredients

4 oz. (110g) butter, softened
2/3 cup + 2 tbsp. of sugar, divided
2 large eggs
1 1/4 cup self-rising flour
1/4 cup cocoa
2 green apples, cored, peeled and chopped
9 oz. (255g) fresh blackberries
2 tbsp. cold water

Method

Preheat oven to 350 ° F (180 °C). Cream butter and 2 cups sugar, then add one egg at a time, followed by 1 tablespoon of flour after each egg and beating well after each addition. Fold in remaining flour and cocoa until well combined. Place the fruit in the base of a casserole dish. Sprinkle with into a 1-quart casserole dish. Sprinkle with 2 tbsp. sugar and cold water. Spread batter over fruit. Bake 45 minutes or until the top is golden brown. Leave to cool at room temperature then wrap and freeze. before wrapping and freezing.

To serve, thaw in the refrigerator for 12 hours. Bake in preheated 350 ° F (180 °C) oven for 30 minutes or until warmed through.

Chocolate Cream Cups

Ingredients
5 1/2 oz. (155g) semisweet chocolate, chopped
2 tbsp. butter, cut into pieces
4 large eggs, separated
1 pinch of salt
1/3 cups of sugar
2/3 cups heavy whipping cream

Method
Melt chocolate and butter in the top of a double boiler pan over simmering water. Remove from heat and set aside to cool at room temperature

Beat the egg whites and the salt into a bowl until stiff peaks form. Gradually add sugar beating well after each addition. Once the chocolate has cooled, add the egg yolks one at a time, stirring well after each addition. Fold the egg white mixture into the chocolate mixture.

In a separate bowl, beat the heavy whipping cream until soft peaks form.

Spoon the chocolate mixture into 6 small 1/2 cup capacity freezer containers, ensuring each container is 2/3 full. Fill the rest of each container with whipped cream. Place cups in the freezer until set. Wrap well and return to the freezer.

To serve, thaw at room temperature.

Apple Cinnamon Tart

Ingredients

4 Granny Smith apples, cored, peeled and sliced
3 tbsp. of sugar
1 tbsp. cinnamon
1 tbsp. butter, cut into pieces
1 pre-baked pie crust.

Method

Preheat oven to 425 °F (220 °C). Combine sugar and cinnamon in a bowl. Add apple pieces and stir until apple is well coated. Place the apple slice overlapping each other in the pre-baked piecrust.

Place pieces of butter over the apples. Bake 12 minutes or until the apples are just starting to caramelize. Leave to cool at room temperature then wrap and freeze. Thaw for 12 hours in the refrigerator before serving.

Cherry Almond Crumble

Ingredients

1 1/4 cup flour
1 cup almonds, ground fine
4 oz. (110g) butter, cut into pieces
1/4 C + 2 tbsp. of sugar, divided
2 lb. (1kg) pitted cherries
2 tbsp. apple juice

Method

Preheat the oven to 350 ° F (180 °C). Combine flour, almonds and butter in a bowl and work the mixture with your fingers until crumbly. Stir in 1/4 cup of sugar. Place the cherries in the base of a baking dish and sprinkle them with remaining sugar and apple juice, stirring to coat well. Cover with the crumble topping. Bake 30 minutes or until golden brown. Allow to cool, then wrap and freeze. Thaw for 12 hours in refrigerator and heat in oven at 350 ° F (180 °C) for 25 minutes.

Pineapple Cake

Ingredients

2 tbsp. light corn syrup
1 (14 oz./395 g) can of pineapple rings, drained
10 tbsp. butter, room temperature
2/3 cups of sugar
2 large eggs
1 1/2 cup self-rising flour
3 tbsp. of milk

Method

Preheat oven to 350 ° F (180 °C). Drizzle the syrup over the base of a greased baking dish. Place the pineapple rings over the syrup (do not allow them to overlap).
Cream butter and sugar, then beat in the eggs one at a time. Stir in remaining flour, then add the milk gradually, mixing well after each addition until the mixture forms a light dough.
Pour the mixture evenly over the top of the pineapple. Bake 25 minutes.
Set aside to cool at room temperature then wrap and freeze.
To serve, thaw completely then heat in a preheated 350 ° F (180 °C) oven for about 10 minutes.

Homemade Pecan Freezer Pie

Ingredients

4 oz. (110g) butter
2 tbsp. of light corn syrup
1/3 cup light brown sugar, packed
1/3 cup dark brown sugar, packed
2 1/2 cup pecan halves
2 large eggs, lightly beaten
1 pie-crust, pre-baked

Method

Preheat oven to 400 °F (205 °C).
Combine butter and syrup in a saucepan and stir constantly over low heat until melted.
Remove the pan from the heat and add all sugar, stirring until sugar dissolves. Fold in the pecans and stir to coat. Add both eggs and combine well.
Pour the mixture into the prepared pie crust. Bake 35 minutes. Cool at room temperature and then wrap and freeze.
Thaw pie in refrigerator for 12 hours before serving.

Freezer Meal FAQs

Can I freeze cooked green beans and peas?

Vegetables freeze best when blanched or raw. Cooked beans and peas might lose their texture in between the freezing and thawing process. For best results, blanch them by dunking the vegetables in boiling water and then quickly immersing them in ice-cold water. Wait until they return to room temperature before freezing.

Freezing vegetables while they are in season is a great way to keep these vegetables on hand throughout the year, without having to pay astronomical prices for out-of-season stock.

Can I freeze cheese?

Yes, you can always have cheese on hand if you keep supplies in the freezer. Slice or grate your cheese before freezing as a block of cheese tends to crumble upon thawing and it can be difficult to slice. Frozen grated cheese is particularly handy as you can use it straight from the freezer to sprinkle over pizzas or stir into a sauce.

I enjoy making my own bread occasionally. If I made extra home-made dough, could I freeze the dough to bake later?

Yes, home-made dough freezes very well although you need to take a few extra precautions to ensure it rises properly when you are ready to bake. First of all, double the amount of yeast in the recipe, to compensate for any yeast dying off during the freezing process. Only use active dry yeast rather than fast-acting yeast. Allow the bread to rise once then form it into a loaf and wrap it tightly before freezing. Thaw at room temperature. Rework the dough and allow it to rise once more before baking.

Can I freeze individual meals of pasta and spaghetti sauce?
The spaghetti sauce will freeze beautifully but the pasta will lose its texture during the freezing process. Your best option is to freeze the pasta sauce in individual/ family size servings, then cook the pasta while it is defrosting. You can thaw spaghetti sauce at room temperature or in the microwave if you wish. Once it is sufficiently thawed, you can warm it up in a pan over the stove to ensure it heats evenly.

What does "flash freeze" mean?
"Flash freeze" means you partially freeze an individual item, such as a cookie, before packing it with all the other flash-frozen cookies. Flash freezing prevents the individual items meshing together as they freeze. You can flash freeze at home by placing the individual items on a cookie tray so they are not touching, and freeze them for a short time.

Can I freeze fruit to use for smoothies?
Using frozen fruit for smoothies is an excellent option. Flash-freeze berries, sliced apples or sliced peaches before packing together, so you can take out a handful of frozen fruit each time, rather than thawing out a whole container. You can also freeze mashed banana, to use in smoothies or baking.

How can I freeze potatoes so they don't lose their texture and flavor when they are thawed?
Potatoes do not generally freeze well as the added moisture disturbs the texture. For casseroles and soups with potato pieces, you would do better to add the potato after thawing. One possible exception to the potato rule is mashed potato, so long as it is frozen separately. Careful thawing and

reheating can remove the excess moisture without spoiling the texture of the potato.

Can I freeze chocolate or candy?
If you use cooking chocolate for baking and sauces, then freezing your supplies is a great way to keep it on hand. You will notice some change in appearance when the chocolate is thawed, which may make the chocolate less tempting to nibble on, but do not affect its quality as an ingredient. Freezing chocolate accelerates the crystallization process, which in turn will upset the balance between the key components, water, fat and sugar. This will have some effect on the external appearance of the chocolate.
Hard candy can be flash-frozen and then stored in the freezer. It is a great way to avoid temptation!

Made in the USA
Monee, IL
21 March 2020